CELEBRATING BRIGHTON & HOVE

KEVIN NEWMAN

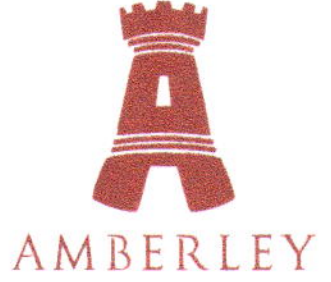

AMBERLEY

First published 2021

Amberley Publishing, The Hill, Stroud
Gloucestershire GL5 4EP

www.amberley-books.com

British Library Cataloguing in Publication Data.
A catalogue record for this book is available from the British Library.

ISBN 978 1 3981 0020 6 (print)
ISBN 978 1 3981 0021 3 (ebook)

Typesetting by SJmagic DESIGN SERVICES, India.
Printed in Great Britain.

Contents

Introduction 4

1   Amazing Authors 9

2   Anniversaries 14

3   Celebrations Across the Centuries 16

4   Wartime Brighton and Hove 18

5   Famous For and Firsts 32

6   Health and Wealth 41

7   Ideas, Inventions and Inventors 50

8   Local Heroes 59

9   Local Traditions 73

10   Pageants, Fairs, Festivals and Fun 76

11   Royal Visits 81

12   Sporting Successes 89

13   A Selection of Societies and Collection of Clubs 92

Acknowledgements 96

About the Author 96

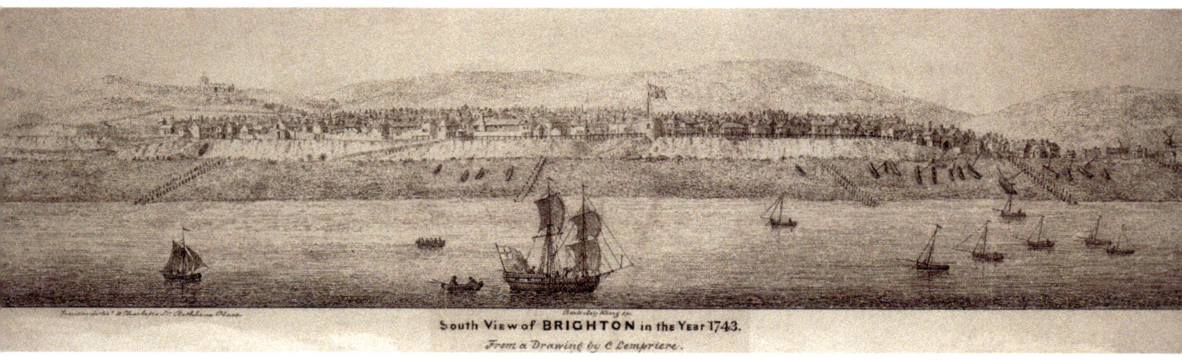

South view of Brighton, 1743.

Introduction

Brighton is interesting only in its past. To-day it is a suburb, a lung, of London; the rapid recuperator of Londoners with whom the pace has been too severe; the Mecca of day-excursionists.

E. V. Lucas, *Highways and Byways in Sussex* (1904)

It is hard to agree with Lucas in relation to present-day Brighton and Hove, which has many offerings from both the past and the present. How can you not find fascinating a place that has been inhabited since 3000 BC? A place whose estimated 100 billion pebbles make a world-famous beach, stretched across 5.4 miles of coastline. Brighton is fascinating both above and below ground. Below the city we have 13,600 miles of sewers, some of which you can visit. Strangely, though, we have only 8,070 miles of water mains – suggesting an unhealthy relationship between what we consume and create! Above ground we are enclosed

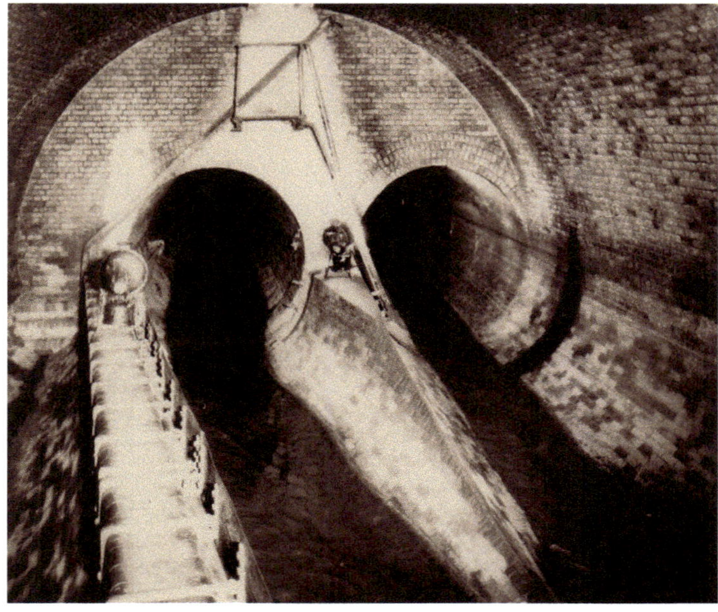

Brighton's sewers.

largely by the Downs and the sea. We are still the rarity of seaside locations, however, being a city with 10,000 acres of council-owned farm and farmlands, and ninety-eight parks and public open spaces. Despite its green backdrop of the Downs we are still very much a city, with inner-city levels of pollution on some of our 3,000-plus roads and twenty-first-century levels of traffic crammed into a settlement that started accelerated growth in the eighteenth century. The historic centre of the Lanes of course cannot even fit cars. Brighton has therefore become a car-unfriendly city, despite its motoring heritage. It is now a pathfinder in terms of public and environmentally friendly transport, which copes with its almost 11 million visits a year. We are therefore worth celebrating as a city of contrasts.

Lucas was correct, though, still in that out of these near 11 million, 9.4 million are day trippers. Even today the city's tourism bosses and business leaders still ponder how to make those stays last longer. Yet he is wrong about the modern city, as it is our past *and* present that brings such huge visitor numbers. People come for Pride and the Great Escape festival, as well as Brighton Pavilion and the city's architecture. Lucas's comment is perhaps partially understandable as he was writing at a time – 1904 – when Brighton's two central hotels, the Royal York and Royal Albion, were neglected and he would not have seen the numerous

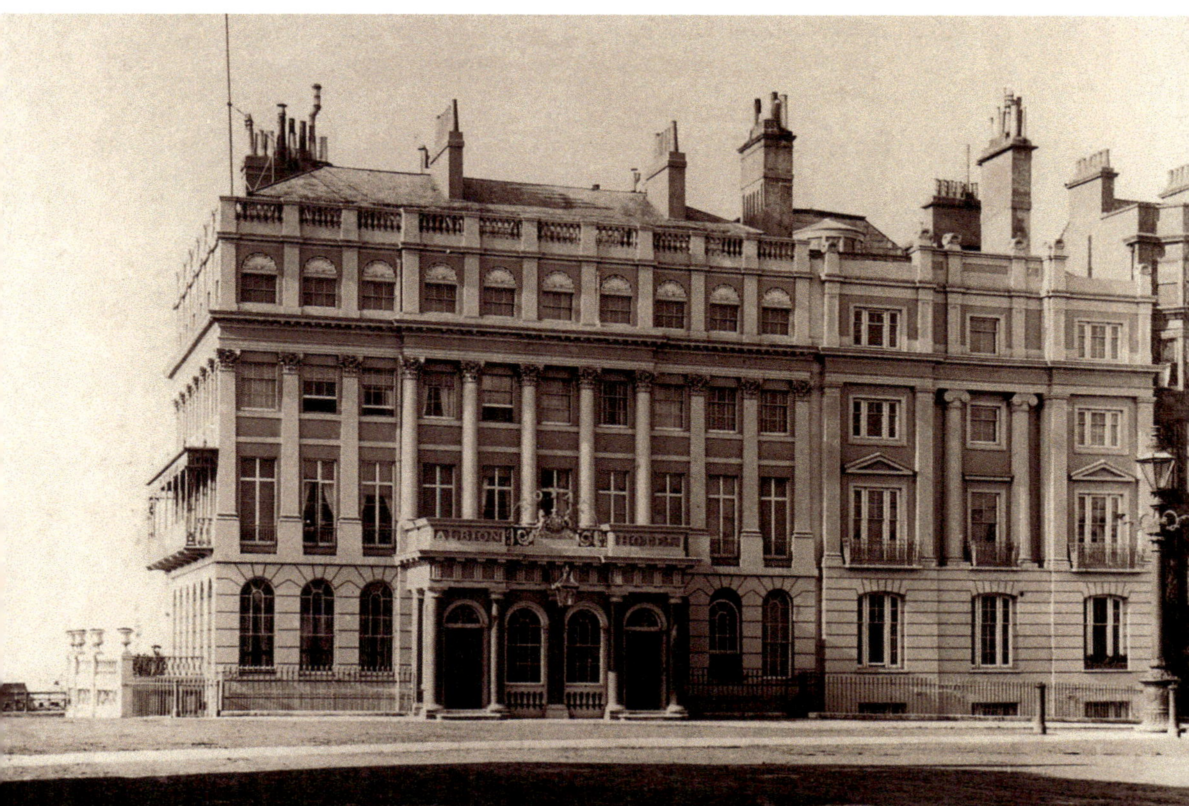

The Royal Albion Hotel.

rejuvenations and reinventions the town (and later on city) would go through. He probably wouldn't like the place today and he certainly might not have liked Brighton in 1904, but he liked its location, as we will see.

I hope in reading *Celebrating Brighton & Hove* you will, unlike Lucas, come to appreciate both Brighton and Hove in its past and its present, as it is Brighton's past that makes it what it is today. How can you not celebrate a city whose greatest strength since the mid-eighteenth century has been its ethos of welcoming everyone – whatever sexuality and whether the monarchy, aristocracy, day trippers, festival goers, conference delegates, holidaymakers, London escapers, creative entrepreneurs or students from home or abroad. Brighton experiences the greatest number of European visitors of any British seaside city. It is little wonder that the two stone pillars in the middle and eastern side of the A23 that welcome you as you enter Greater Brighton have the following engraving on them: 'HAIL GUEST, WE ASK NOT WHAT THOU ART. IF FRIEND, WE GREET THEE HAND & HEART. IF STRANGER, SUCH NO LONGER BE. IF FOE, OUR LOVE SHALL CONQUER THEE.'

Brighton has also welcomed those of religion and those of none. It experienced a huge boom in church building in the nineteenth century, with the Wagner family, who built the amazing St Bartholomew's Church, and others at the forefront of proceedings back then. We are reminded of the strength of Brighton's religious community at this time by the way that even our clock towers encourage us to worship God. On the eastern side of Preston Park, the red-brick and terracotta clock tower (1890s) has the following engraving: 'Here I stand with all my might to tell the hour by day and night. Therefore example take by me and serve thy God as I serve thee.' If, however, you lack religious conviction, like me, then you could have journeyed to the Chain Pier, which stood from 1823 to 1896. There you could have taken in the poet Richard Henry Horne's line 'Tis always morning somewhere in the world', which was engraved on the sundial at the landing end of the pier. He was indeed correct.

We need to celebrate Brighthelmstonians, Brightonians and Hovites across the centuries too – they were survivors. The earliest inhabitants of the town would probably have had to survive raids by the Saxons, Vikings and French, and then endure countless batterings from the elements. An old belief was that an early Brighton settlement – probably on the beach again – was swept away and submerged by the sea in a great storm of 1278, the same year the original port of Winchelsea down the coast was also destroyed. The Anglo-Saxon Chronicle, one of our earliest historical records, notes that Brighthelmstone faced 'bad wind' in 1103, 1114, 1118 and 1121. The year 1348 saw not only the plague sweeping Britain, but Brighton also faced yet another storm. A total of 100 houses were destroyed in one night in the 1700s when Brighton lost South Street (it was replaced by today's King's Road) and much of Hove was washed away too. These people were tough. They needed to be to survive malnutrition, the elements, Vikings and the waves.

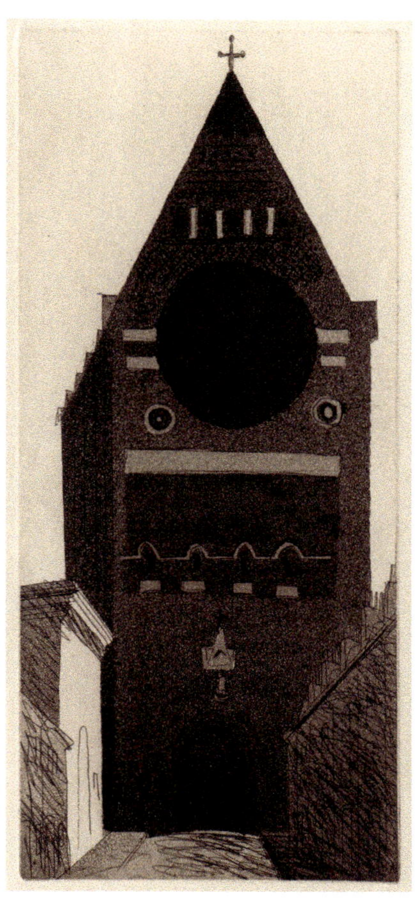

Right: St Bartholomew's Church.

Below: Preston Park Clock Tower.

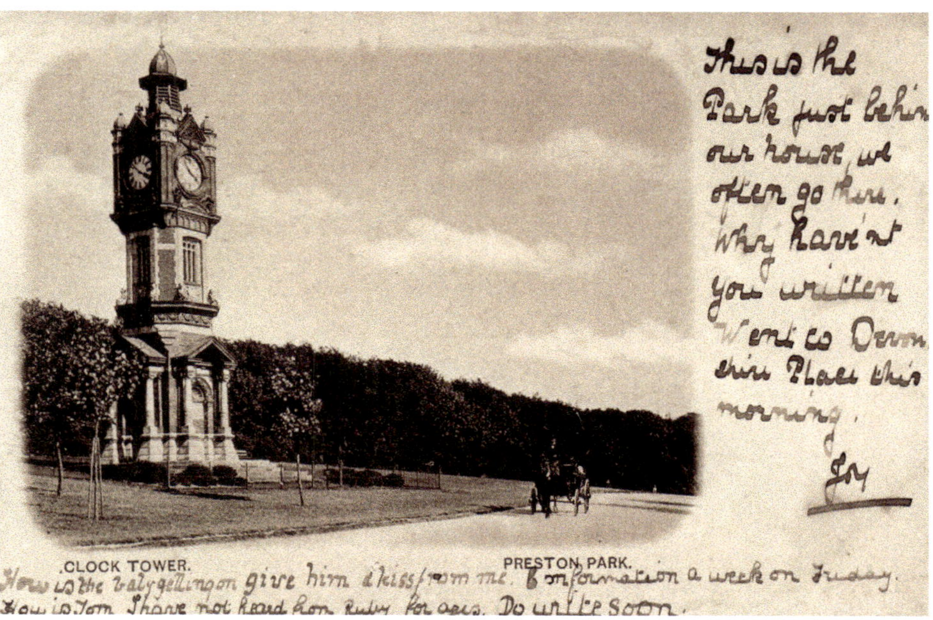

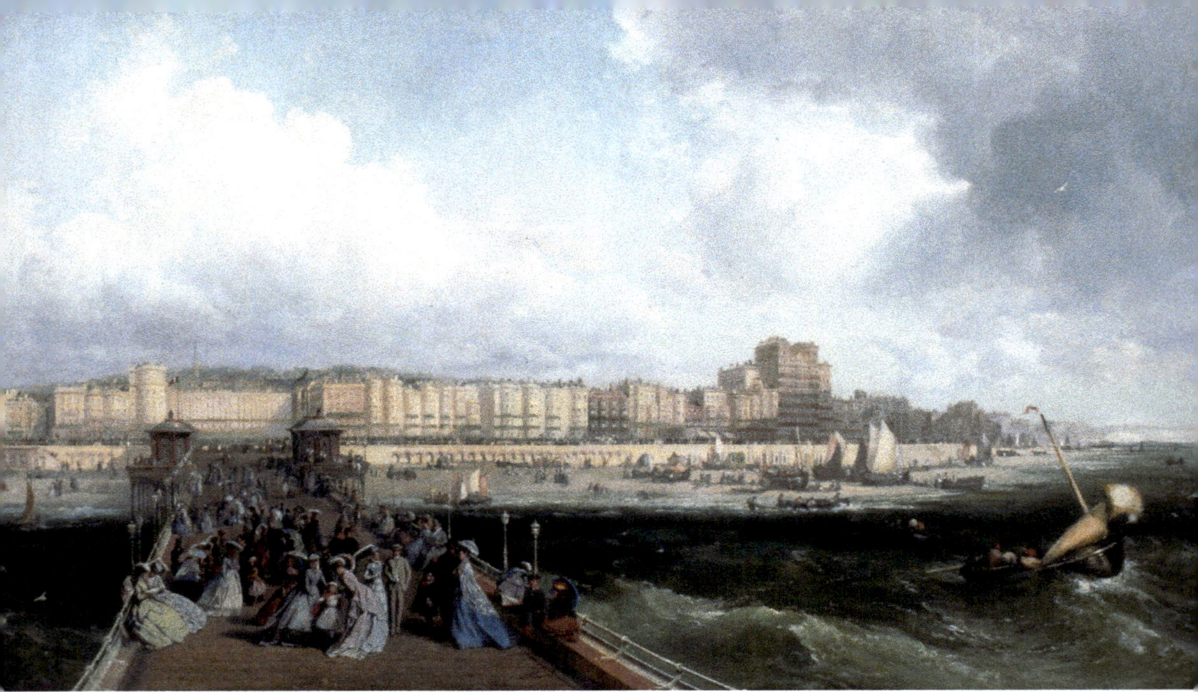

Celebrating Brighton & Hove aims to showcase the positive people, amazing animals and exciting events of Sussex's premier city – from its past up to the present. It takes a cheeky, sneaky peak at the historical celebrations of yesteryear, at remarkable local people, notable events and feats of great achievement and ambition. It celebrates the people and places that make Brighton and Hove unique, vibrant and irresistible to visitors. How could you disagree with the verdict of Martin Sirk, Brighton Council's Conference Officer in 1991, who summed us up as 'Cleaner than London and Birmingham, [with a] better atmosphere than Bournemouth' and 'not as tidy as Harrogate but a lot less boring'?

So many history books focus on what is lost, but *Celebrating Brighton & Hove* explores traditions touching today, and investigates industry and entrepreneurs who have provided employment and prosperity. It finds festivals and events that Brighton and Hove hosts, and tells of local heroes and benefactors, as well as heart-warming stories of restoration and rejuvenation in addition to Brighton and Hove's 'firsts'.

Celebrating Brighton & Hove provides a miscellany of greatness, detailing the history of how and what makes this seaside city so iconic and worth celebrating. Lucas may have been partly correct that much of Brighton's brilliance was in its past, but the fact that so many of the 11 million who visit today do so because of our past suggests that the past has mostly survived into the future, and with all the city's many strengths and eccentricities today it truly makes it a place worth celebrating.

Note: Where I am referring to Brighton or Hove pre-2000 I use the term 'town' and after 2000, when the two were joined as a city, that term is used instead.

Amazing Authors

Being such an iconic location, with its legendary views and seashore, Brighton and neighbouring Hove have unsurprisingly attracted a huge range of literary talent over the years. The city's hotels have provided the peace and solitude necessary for writing, the romance of the city has inspired many, and a number of authors have made their home here. We cannot hope to cover everyone in this section as space is limited, but we shall look at some major writers who have stayed here and some locations you can visit.

Hove has had a huge range of famous people schooled in its streets, which might also help explain its literary heritage. In 1841 it had ten schools, and this increased to a peak of thirty-eight in 1871 – remarkable for a small town. Its beneficial climate, sea air, good drainage and 'perfect sanitary arrangements' were used as factors to get a range of children to the town, including none other than soldier, politician, prime minister and, of course, author Winston Churchill. His heath

The beach at Brunswick Square.

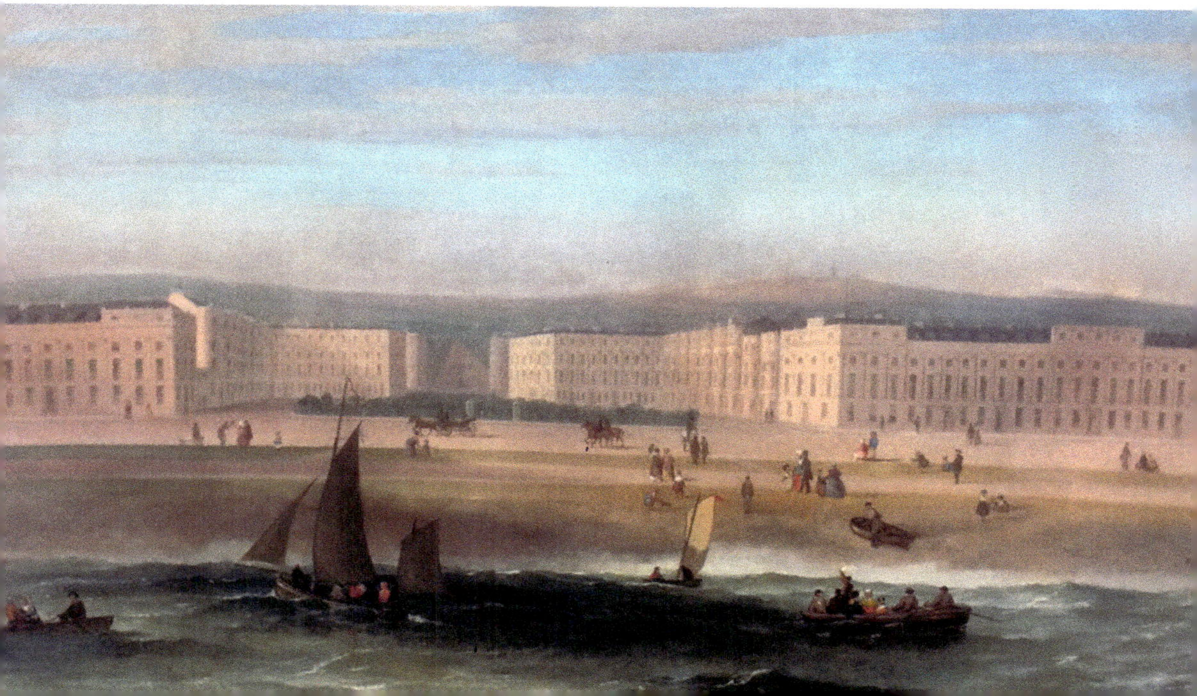

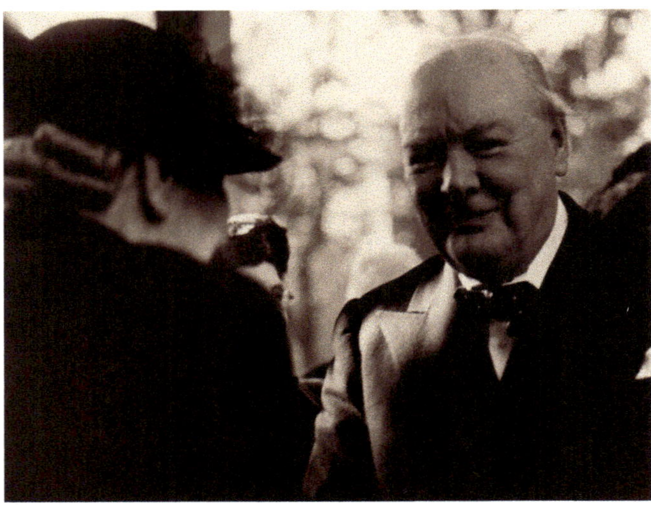

Winston Churchill visiting in 1947 when he was made a freeman of the town.

improved dramatically here once he recovered from a serious bout of the flu. Having the family doctor (who lived in the town) at his bedside must have helped.

Graham Greene saluted Patrick Hamilton's *The West Pier* as 'The best book written about Brighton'. Hamilton grew up in Hove, attending Holland Road School, and went on to write *The West Pier* trilogy, a truly chilling set of books about a psychopath. Churchill himself had a chilling incident between 1883 and 1885 while he was a pupil at the school at Nos 29–30 Brunswick Road, on the corner of Lansdowne Road. An argument with another pupil over a penknife led to the future prime minister being stabbed. Thankfully, the blade only penetrated an inch and did no lasting damage. His later visits, when he stayed at the Hotel Metropole, were thankfully more peaceful.

Hotels play a prominent part in our hosting of authors, as you'd expect; but they are also the sites used for fictional characters in Brighton-based novels too. Charles Dickens Jr, son of the famous author, stayed in Brighton in 1891 (decades after his father's death) to rest after a series of lectures. Dickens Jr preferred the Metropole, whereas his father famously stayed in the Bedford, which burned down seventy years later in the 1960s. Dickens Sr also stayed at the Old Ship in February 1841, which was the year *The Old Curiosity Shop* and *Barnaby Rudge* came out. He gave readings of his novels from the Old Ship and Royal York hotel (the YHA today) and at the Town Hall. In 1860 *David Copperfield* was also read by Dickens Sr to audiences at the Royal York.

Both authors and their literary creations seem to be fond of the town. George Osborne, in William Makepeace Thackeray's novel *Vanity Fair* (published 1847–48), enjoyed his fictional stay at the Old Ship, which might have been due to Thackeray's equally pleasant stay at the hotel, where he wrote parts of *Vanity Fair*. Thackeray also stayed at the Royal York, as did Benjamin Disraeli. Poets Tennyson and Wordsworth also stayed at the Old Ship, which must have been a very different experience from his Lake District wanderings.

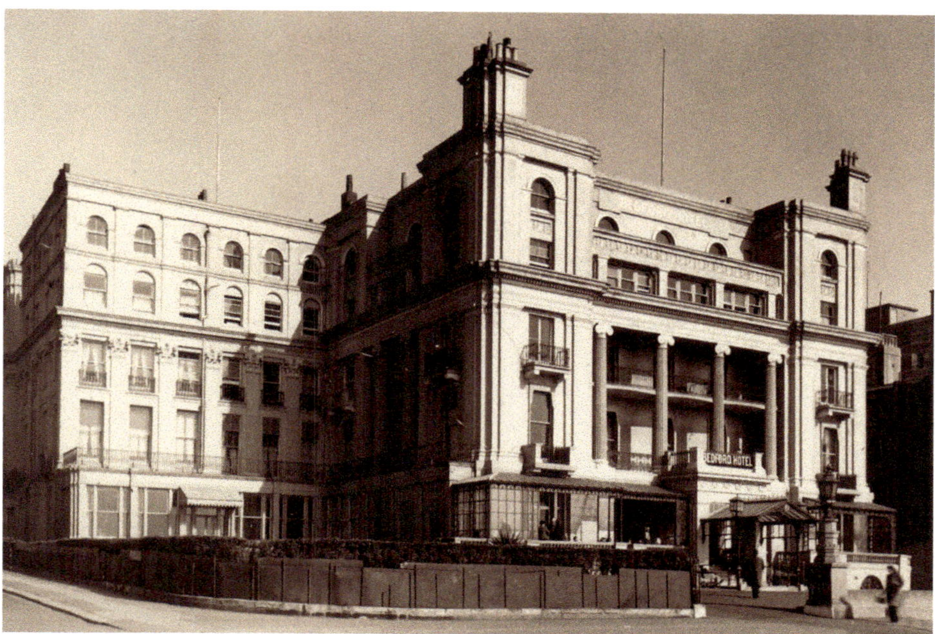

The Bedford Hotel.

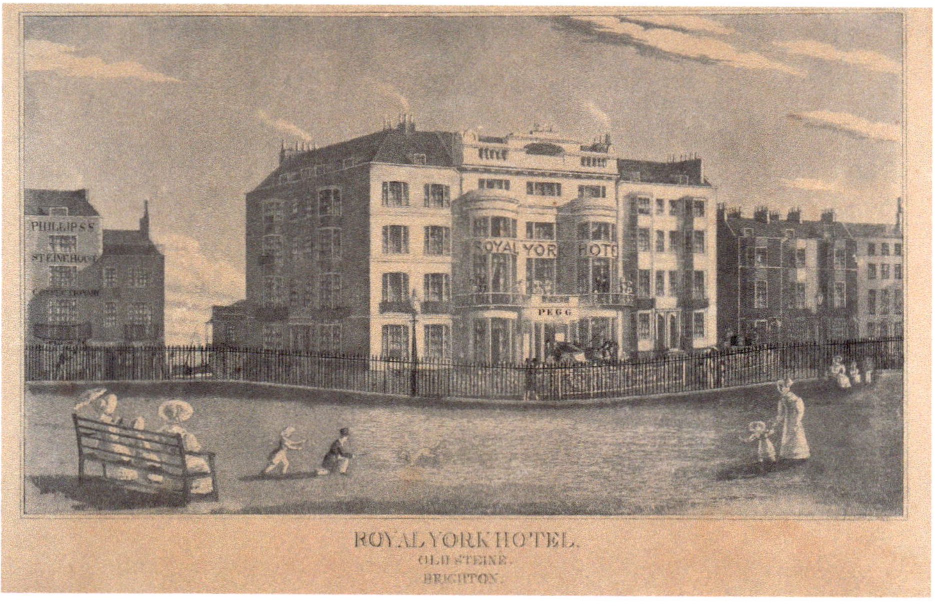

The Royal York Hotel.

Graham Greene's most famous work, *Brighton Rock*, uses Brighton hotels heavily for the location of its dramatic scenes. The town's hotels also grace his other Brighton-based work, *Travels With My Aunt*. Greene featured the Cricketers pub in his work, but he preferred to write at the Royal Albion and the Metropole.

These were also the hotels that Oscar Wilde stayed in during his visits to Brighton. Wilde's antics on his visit to nearby Worthing with the youth Alphonse Conway would lead to his downfall and stay in Reading Gaol, but his time in Brighton wasn't trouble-free either. Wilde managed to crash a horse and cart he and Lord Douglas were driving, and he checked out of the Metropole without paying his bill.

Richard Jefferies (1848–1887), celebrated for his writings on nature, claimed that 'there are more handsome women in Brighton than anywhere else in the world. They are so common that gradually the standard of taste in the mind rises, and good-looking women who would be admired in other places pass without notice'. Jefferies, who actually lived in Hove, even praised Brighton's treelessness, which Samuel Johnson (the famous dictionary author) had once complained about so vigorously. He claimed that Brighton's lack of trees made the place healthier than other resorts. 'Let nothing,' he exclaimed, 'cloud the descent of those glorious beams of sunlight which fall at Brighton. Watch the pebbles on the beach; the foam runs up and wets them, almost before it can slip back, the sunshine has dried them again … Brighton is a Spanish town in England; a Seville.'

E. V. Lucas, despite his belief that Brighton was only interesting in the past (as previously discussed), did rate its location:

The value of Brighton lies in its position as the key to good country. In half an hour one can be at the Dyke [these were the days when you took the railway up to the Dyke] and free of miles of turfed Down or cultivated Weald; in a few minutes one can reach Hassocks, the station for Wolstonbury or Ditchling

Devil's Dyke.

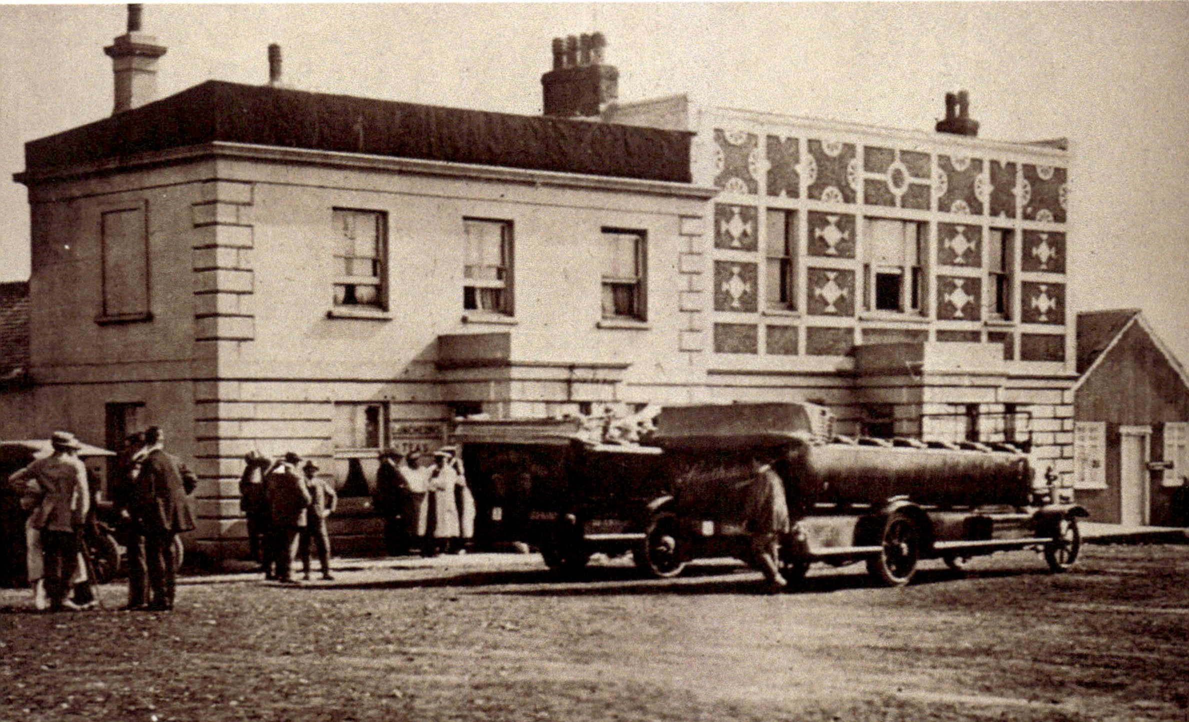

Beacon; in a few minutes one can plunge into Stanmer Park, or correct the effect of Brighton's hard brilliance amid the soothing sleepiness of Lewes; in a few minutes one can be at Shoreham, amid shipbuilders and sailmakers; or on the ramparts of Bramber Castle, or among the distractions of Steyning cattle market, with Chanctonbury ring rising solemnly beyond.

This is all mostly still true today, even with stations at Bramber and the Dyke long gone due to Brighton's good bus network, or via use of a car.

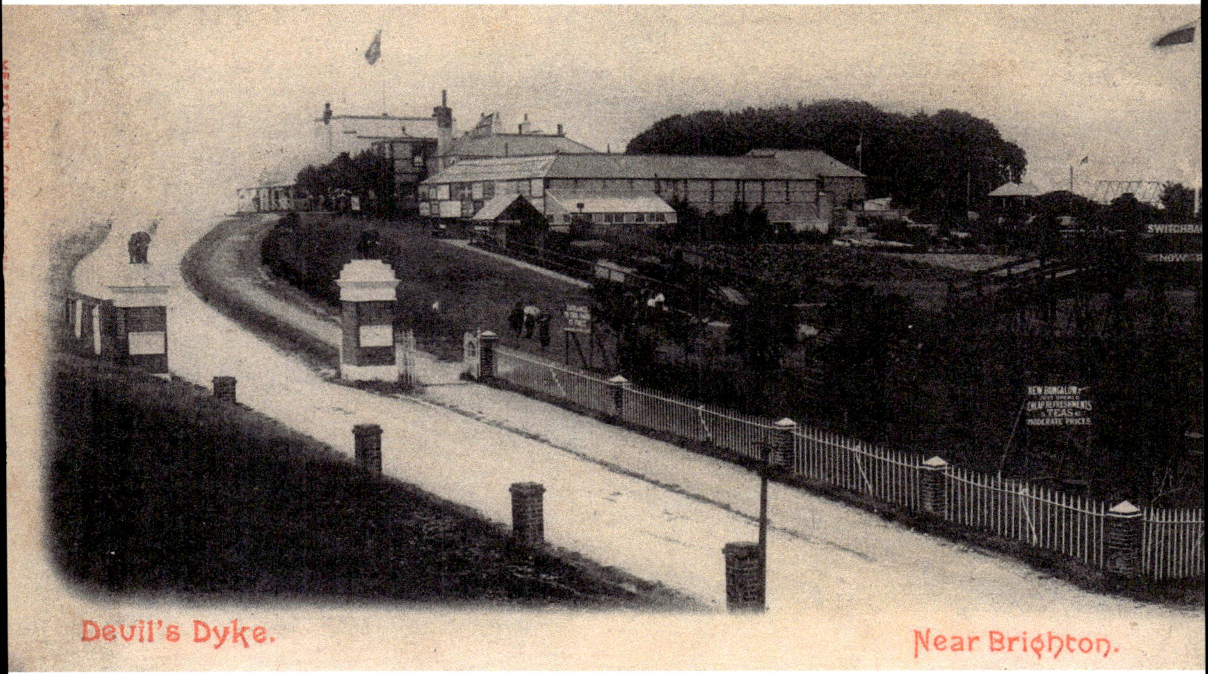

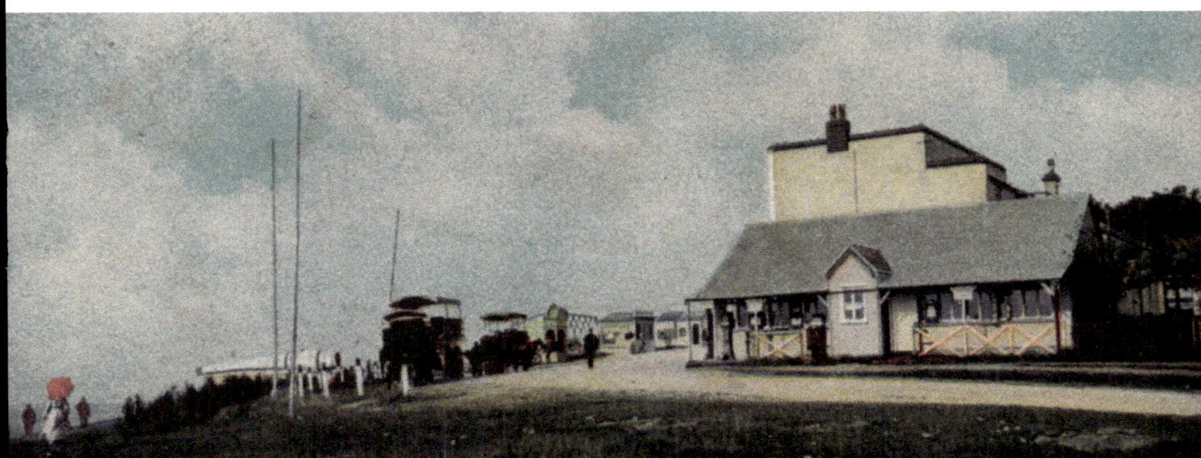

Above: An earlier look at the buildings at Devil's Dyke.

Below: The former Dyke Hotel.

Anniversaries

There were many holy days and other dates in Brighton and Hove where you could engage in a variety of celebrations. Firstly, you had Birds Wedding Day, which was the old Sussex name for St Valentine's Day (14 February). Next, bind days were when tenants of certain manors in Sussex had to work for their lord rather than undertake their own work. Crouchmass was St Helena's Day (18 August) and, talking of ladies, Lady-Tide was the festival around 25 March. At the end of the year was the festival of Goodening, when Sussex folk went around peoples' houses asking for aid on St Thomas's Day (21 December). This would help them provide for the costly forthcoming Christmas season. Slightly earlier was Waygoose, on 23 November, which was a bean feast or celebration on St Clement's Day. During this festival Brighton folk would enjoy a roast leg of pork, boned and stuffed with sage and onions. Fill-Dick was the most racy-sounding date on the calendar, but only meant February in Sussex's past. 'Dick' usually meant 'dyke' in a number of old Sussex references, but in pudding terms could also mean 'dough'.

Hilaire Belloc's birthday (27 July) has – or should have, at least – become Belloc Day, Sussex's very own version of Burns Night. Belloholics (or you can say 'Bellocians', as used by the Belloc Society) celebrate the life of the Sussex bard (which you call him to annoy fans of Kipling!) by drinking fine local ale and eating the simple Sussex fare of bread, bacon and cheese that Belloc lived on. Belloc believed in 'the goodness of God in the drinking of ale, which is a kind of prayer,' and added, 'drinking good ale is a more renowned and glorious act than any other to which a man can lend himself.' Although Belloc's greatest work, *The Four Men: A Farrago*, doesn't venture into Brighton, Belloc himself did on occasions and was partial to a meal at the Metropole.

The second week in Brighton is when the city's historic racecourse starts its three-day August meeting, a tradition that dates back to the late eighteenth century. The farmer who owned the land allowed racing watched by the Prince of Wales (later George IV) to take place in return for the promise of 27 gallons of wine each year. It always follows Goodwood, and for many years formed part of the Sussex fortnight along with Lewes and Fontwell Park. Sadly, Brighton is the last to carry on this tradition, with the racecourse at Lewes closing in 1964 and Fontwell no longer holding summer races of this nature. The races in August include the Brighton Mile, the Brighton Challenge Cup and the Brighton Bullet. The horse Operatic Society won the Challenge Cup in 1960, along with many other races in his long career. As a result, for many years after Brighton held a race, the Operatic Society Challenge Cup, in his memory.

From horses to horsepower. Brighton welcomes a plethora of veteran cars every November to celebrate the lifting of the 1865 Locomotive Act (otherwise known as the Red Flag Act) in November 1896. The first ever race of cars from London to Brighton started that year. It was called the Emancipation Run to celebrate the repeal of the law, which had limited drivers to 4 mph, curbed the development of the British car industry, and insisted that any self-propelled vehicle had a man walk ahead of it waving a red flag. The event originally finished not on Madeira Drive, as it does today, but outside the Metropole. The race later became known as the Veteran Car Run, with the emphasis being that only the earliest vehicles – veteran cars – could take part.

One other Brighton hotel had a hand in bringing this event about, and it was also involved in the publicity for the race back in 1997. On the run up to the event's 101st anniversary on 31 October 1997, an 1899 Fiat trundled into the restaurant at the Old Ship Hotel in Brighton, surprising diners. The event wasn't part of a badly aimed ram raid, but was part of the publicity involving that year's RAC Veteran Car Run from London to Brighton. The Old Ship has been closely linked with the annual race as it was there, in Brighton's oldest hotel, that the idea for a veteran car club was first discussed. The Fiat in question was on loan to the hotel from Lord Montagu's Beaulieu motor museum and, following its arrival, spent a week in the foyer on display. The Old Ship also decided to celebrate the veteran car race with a special cocktail devised by the hotel's head barman. According to the guest relation manager, Maggie King, the cocktail was 'sure to refuel our guests'.

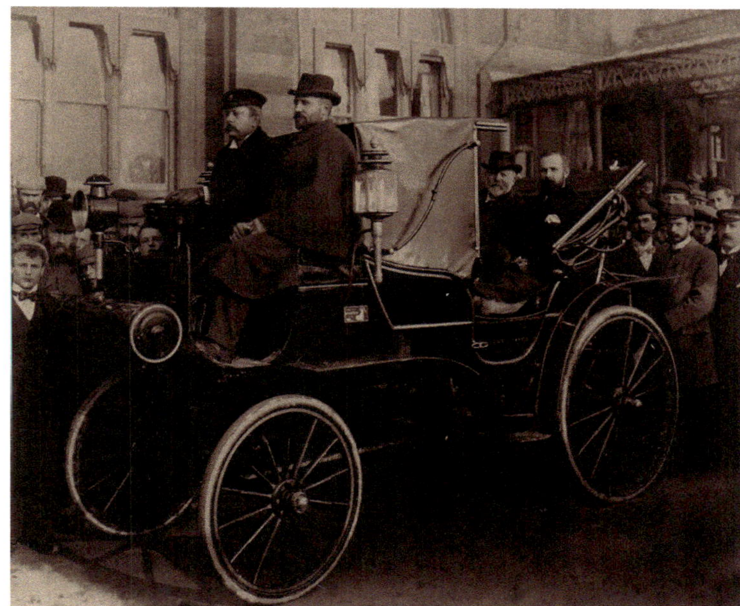

An electric car designed by Magnus Volk outside the Metropole Hotel, Brighton.

Celebrations Across the Centuries

Brighton is the place that people have come to for partying ever since its discovery by the aristocracy in the mid-eighteenth century. Today it is still one of the country's major hotspots for hen nights, stag dos and an all-round party place. Brighton is synonymous with celebrations. A factor that has contributed to this status is that it has had numerous breweries, no doubt helped by Flemish immigrants to the town who brought their country's beer-brewing expertise with them. Brighton's past breweries include the Smithers, Rock and Kemp Town breweries, and it once had the country's biggest 'pub' when the Metropole hosted what was the country's biggest beer festival back in 1987. The Tamplins Brewery in Russell Street (demolished and now in the site of the Churchill Square complex) existed for a fantastic 150 years until the 1960s. It started with one man selling beer from his house and ended up as part of a nationally known brewery. Breweries equalled boozers, and an old Brighton myth was that the place had a pub for every day of the year. That may have been true by the twentieth century, but earlier in 1889 Brighton had 774 pubs – one for every 130 residents, or at least two for every day of the year.

Political party conferences are also a chance for Labour, the Tories and Lib Dems to celebrate, and Brighton has hosted many over the years. Tony Blair's landslide election win in May 1997 meant that the Labour conference in Brighton that September was a massive affair, which entailed many more MPs, supporters and media than usual zooming into town. This then meant a boom for local food and drink providers. The 23,000 visitors brought in £8 million – £5 million more than estimated and double any previous conference. Huge amounts of food and drink had to be brought in to keep the delegates happy, especially at the Grand where most journalists stayed. The hotel served up an amazing 8,000 canapés, 3,000 sandwiches and a hefty 60 kilos of smoked salmon. Ravenous guests chomped an estimated 9,600 eggs, 40 kilos of roast beef and 1,200 kilos of cheese in the 14,600 meals served. With journalists in town, the drink bill was always going to be huge at the Grand, and an estimated £200,000 was spent on 750 bottles of champagne, 3,000 bottles of wine and 10,000 pints of beer.

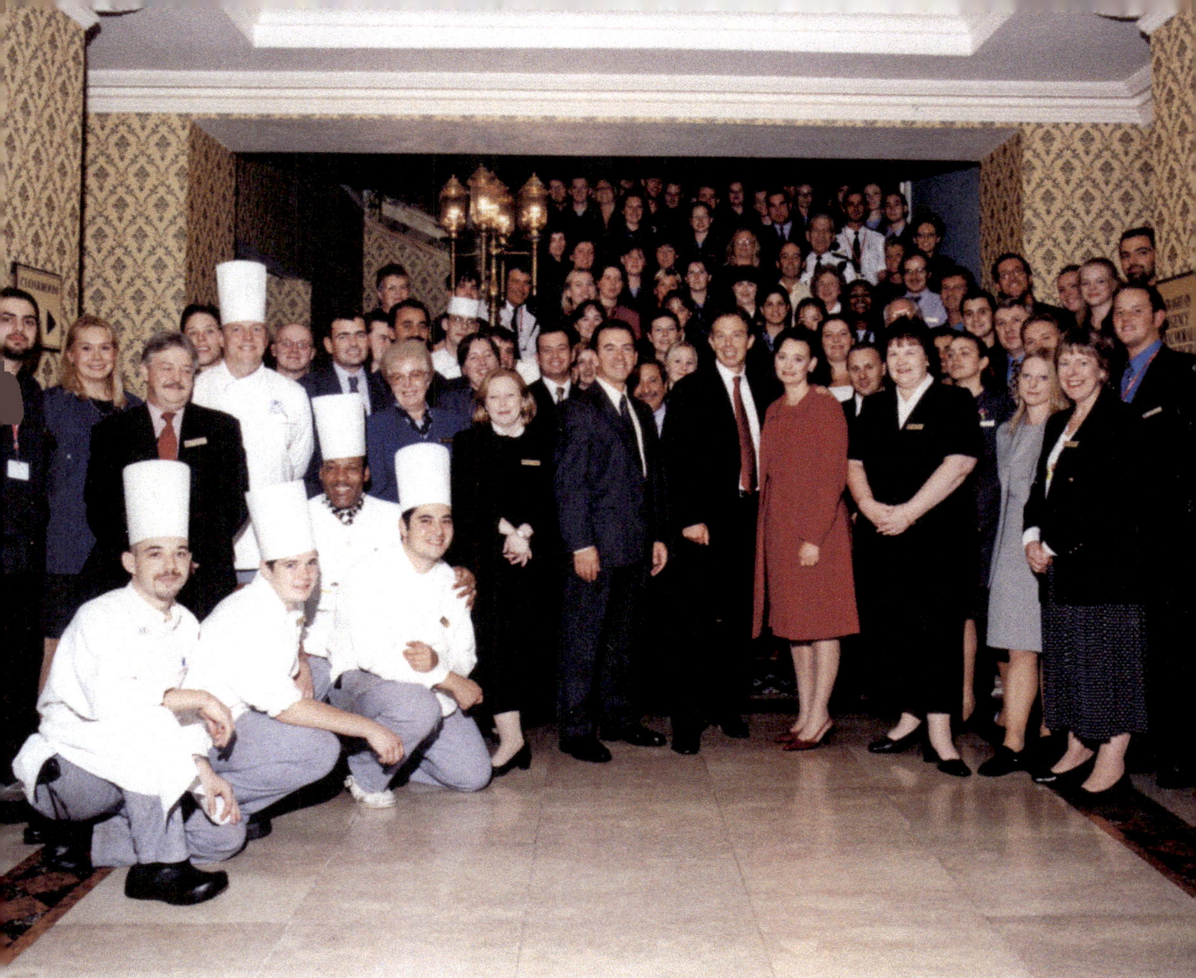

To compare, in a normal week the Grand would serve 220 lb of bacon, 420 loaves of bread and 222 gallons of milk. Staff worked twelve- to fourteen-hour shifts to cater for all of this. The neighbouring Metropole served many more canapés, with 25,000 of the bijou-sized bites being consumed and a whopping 25,000 bottles of wine guzzled throughout the week. This was where Tony Blair and his cabinet were staying, and apparently not all of this was down to John Prescott.

Brighton has probably been celebrated more than any other seaside location in the country, but never until 2017 was the city celebrated by ingredients. This all changed when two Sussex brewers, the Laine Brew Company and Two Tribes brewery, collaborated to produce 'Dirty Weekend'. This aimed to bring beer lovers 'Brighton in a beer glass' and contained melted sticks of Brighton rock, seaweed and even sea salt collected from Brighton Beach. Laine Brewing Company head brewer Nic Donald said, 'All the hops have been chosen as aspects of Brighton's personality. The colour of the beer is the kind of red you get as the suns sets. We wanted the beer to sum up the experience of drinking on the beach in Brighton.' Presumably, it then has to be drunk while crammed together with thousands of Londoners, dubious smoke wafting over you and people being sick nearby.

4

Wartime Brighton and Hove

Wars are and have been the focus of more than enough bookshelves in your local Waterstones or WH Smiths so here we celebrate just the light-hearted and beneficial side of wartime life in Brighton and Hove.

Despite its lack of a harbour, Brighton's beaches were officially a port back in 1805. This meant Brighton was the first place in the UK to announce the victory at Trafalgar and the death of Nelson (it was announced from the Pavilion). Brighton and Hove had another different type of port just over a century later: Shoreham Airport. Brighton and Hove City Airport (as it is known today) was one of the few

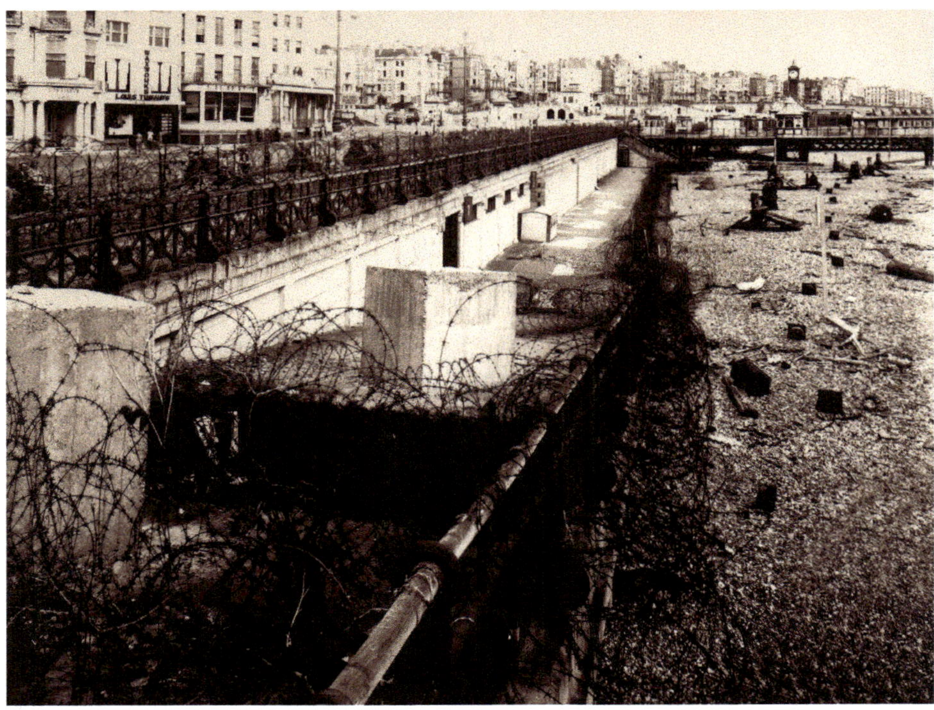

Wartime Brighton.

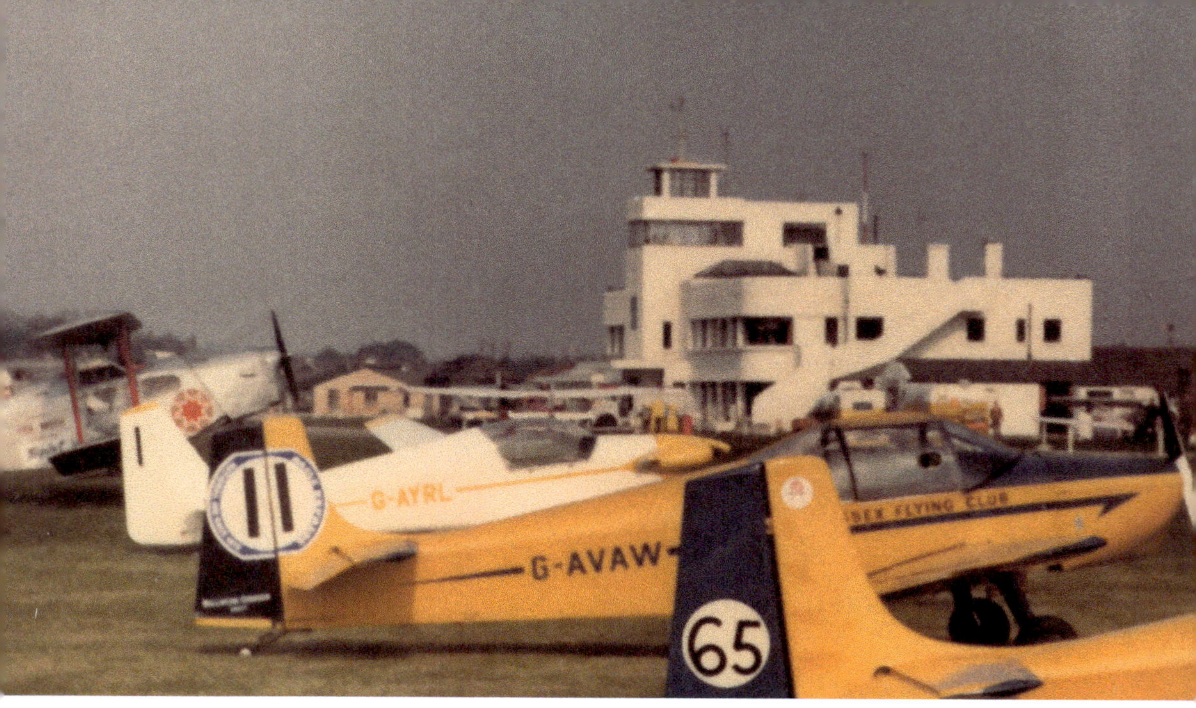

Brighton City Airport (also known as Shoreham Airport).

airfields that some of the Royal Flying Corps (predecessor of the RAF) embarked from for military service in France in 1914. Not all of them completed the journey. Some were reputedly have said to have ended up flying backwards when windspeeds proved to be stronger than the horsepower of the engines. Shoreham was also expected to defend London from the threat from Germany – with one bomber! The airport today rightly celebrates its long heritage as it is one of the earliest centres of aviation in the world, having been continually in use since 1910. It is even the location of the first recorded cargo flight (a box of light bulbs). The famous Cecil and Eric Pashley (still commemorated at the airport) moved their flying club from Brooklands to Shoreham in 1913, but then left it behind in 1914 as they moved into war service. The airport then became an important training centre in the First World War, even claiming to be there at the creation of the Canadian Air Force.

Brighton has a unique construction on the hills above the city, and another in town, celebrating the wartime service of a nation whose efforts were vital and whose numbers of servicemen were significant. Meaning 'umbrella' in Hindi, Punjabi and Urdu, the Chattri is Brighton's memorial and war grave for Sikh and Hindu Indian soldiers who died in Brighton following injuries gained fighting in the First World War for Britain. The Pavilion was where some of them were treated, first between 1914 and 1915 and then between 1916 and 1918 when it became a hospital for soldiers who had lost limbs. It was believed for many years that George V ordered his family's former holiday home to be loaned as an Indian hospital, but as the Pavilion was owned by the Corporation of Brighton (Brighton and Hove Council today) it was actually the decision of Sir Walter Laurence, a local civil servant. For a time the Corporation were also considering converting

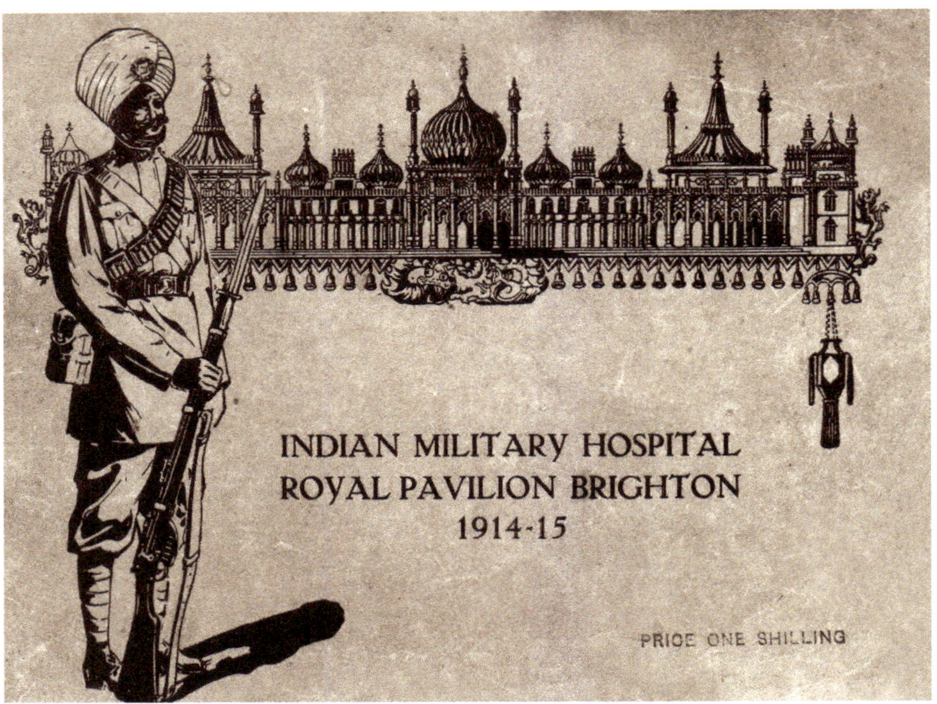

An Indian soldier in a leaflet from the First World War.

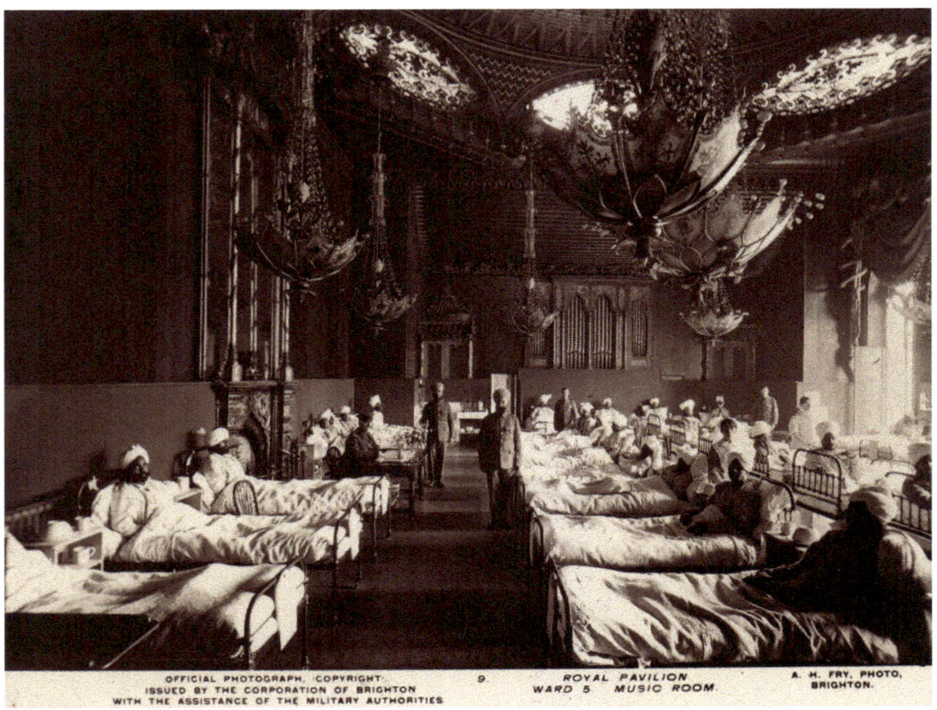

Indian soldiers in beds in the music room of the Royal Pavilion.

Brighton's hotels and even its piers into hospitals, so injured soldiers would have convalesced above the waves had the latter gone ahead. The decision to use the Pavilion and Dome was said to be due to the Indianesque look of the buildings making soldiers from India feel at home; however, since the Pavilion's interior has more of a Chinese aesthetic the decision wasn't the most logical. The Dome also needed some conversion as in 1914 it still had its horse trough in the centre from its days as George IV's riding school and stables.

The hotels and piers were kept out of military medical hands in the First World War (the hotels were deemed too profitable), so the Dome and Pavilion earned their place along with Brighton and Hove's many other war hospitals. The Sikh and Hindu soldiers that died there of their wounds needed a very special Brighton landmark and they got one indeed in the Chattri, which can be seen from the A27 up on the Downs, north of Patcham. The white, dome-topped construction on top of its white steps and platform is now officially looked after by the Commonwealth War Graves Commission. It lists all the names of the soldiers who were cremated and is a poignant reminder of the sacrifice made by the 1 million Indian soldiers who fought for the British Empire in the First World War. It was unveiled in 1921 in an opening ceremony by the then Prince of Wales. The same year the Pavilion's southern gate in East Street was replaced by the gift of the India

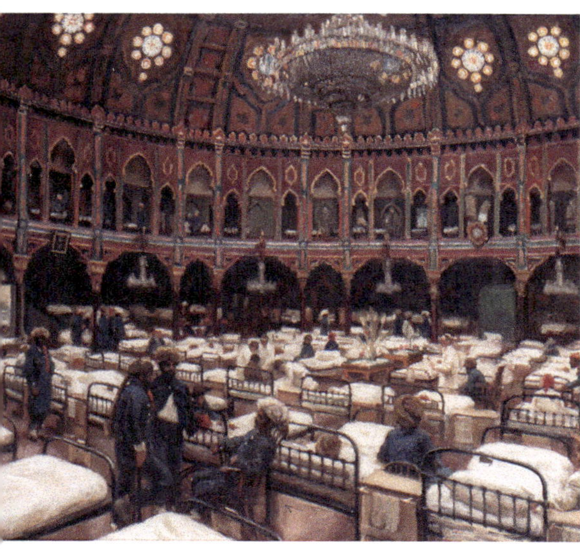

Above: The Dome as an Indian military hospital.

Right: The music room of the Royal Pavilion being used as a hospital for Indian soldiers.

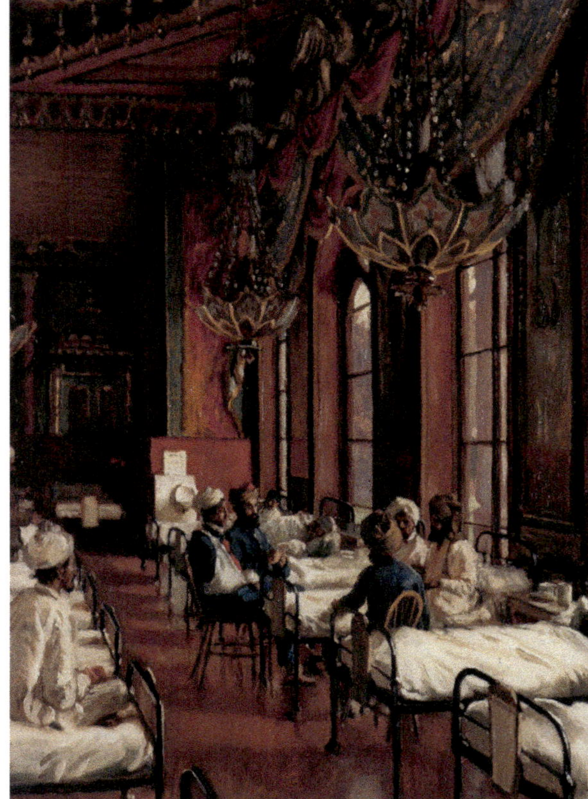

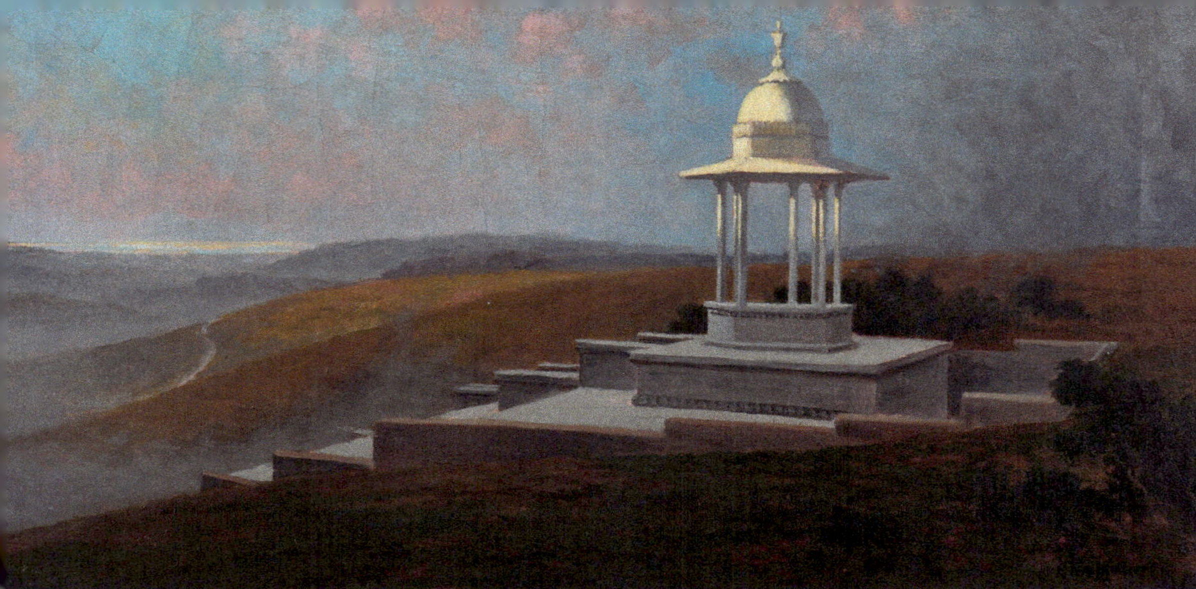

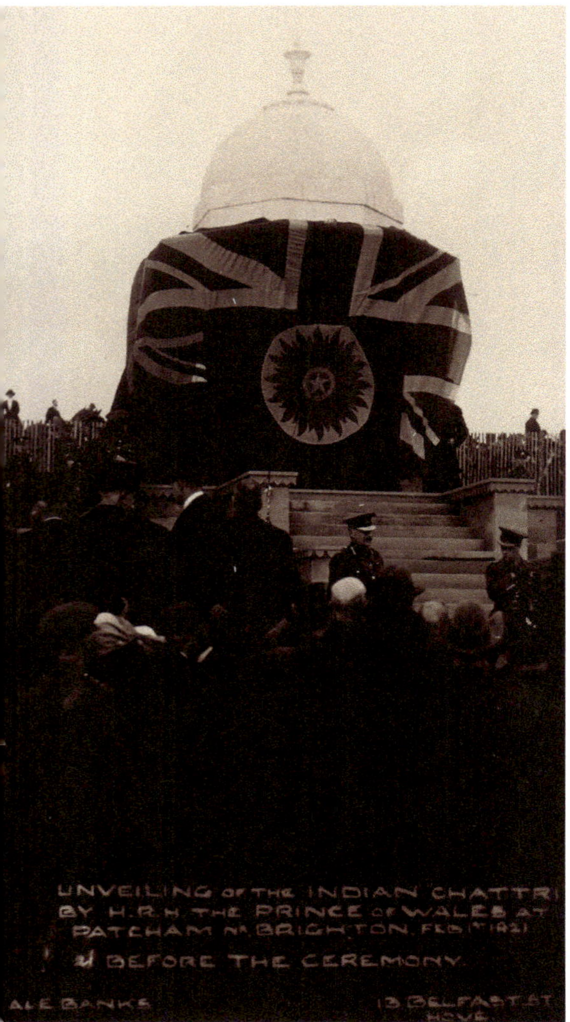

Above: An oil painting of the Chattri, Patcham, by Clem Lambert, *c*. 1920.

Left: Unveiling of the Indian Chattri, 1 February 1921.

Gate in a gesture of thanks from the people of India to the people of Brighton for their care given to Indian soldiers during the war. Like the Chattri, it also ensures the people of Brighton don't forget the bravery of the Indian soldiers who fought, and in many cases died, thousands of miles away from home. These soldiers gave so much and still wanted to say thanks for their care, so it was more than fair that the Maharaja of Patiala, who officially unveiled the gate on Wednesday 26 October 1921, was presented with a gold replica key to Brighton's most famous Indianesque building – the Royal Pavilion. The Maharaja mentioned

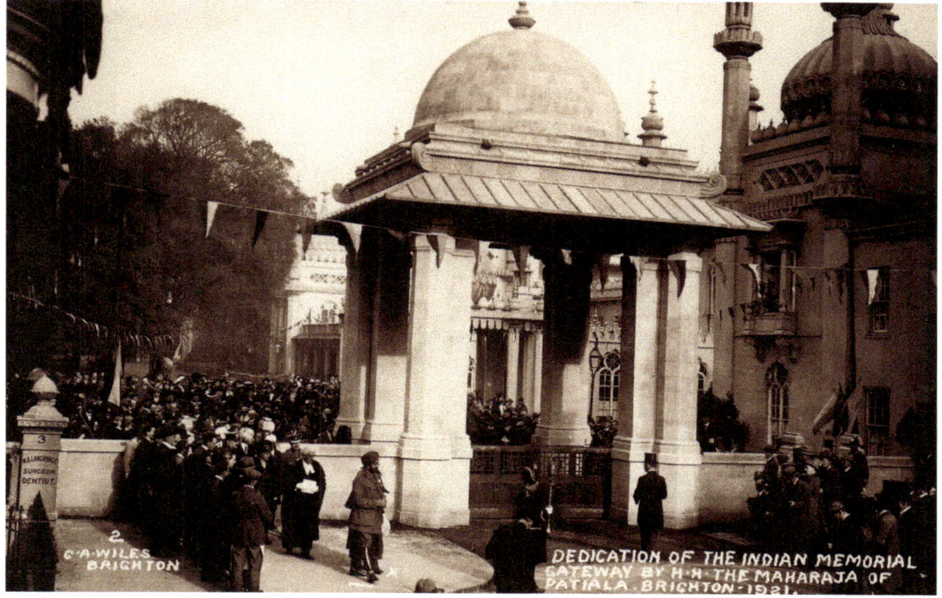

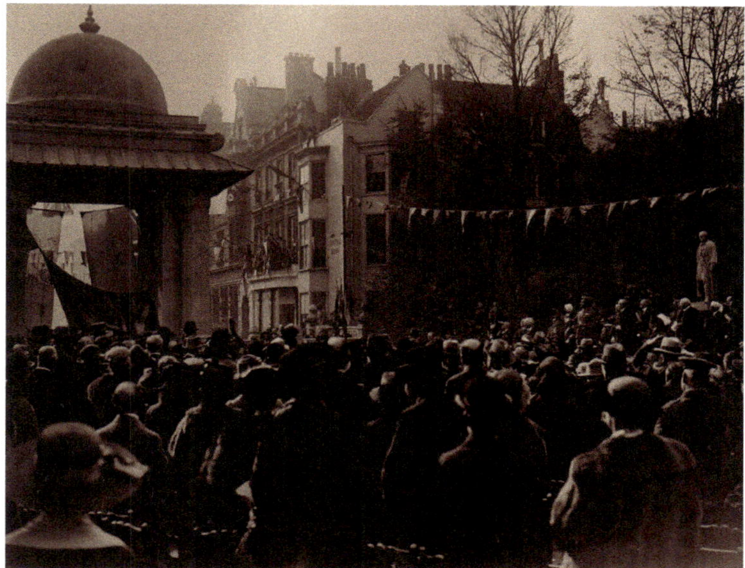

Above and right: Unveiling of the Indian gate, 1921.

at the ceremony how Brighton's name of 'Doctor Brighton' (it being a place of healing at that time) had now spread to even the remotest of Indian villages.

Both the Chattri and its sister monument the India Gate are now treasured monuments of Anglo-Indian relations, with the Chattri being a Grade II listed building. This wasn't always the case though, as sadly in the Second World War the Chattri ended up briefly being used for target practice – some of the marks can still be seen. Today this would never be tolerated, and a memorial service is held there every year to remember these gallant soldiers. You too can easily walk there, using bridle paths and following the signs heading north from Braepool, north of the A27 at Patcham, or by heading southwards from the Jack and Jill windmills at Clayton. Brightonians wanted to inspect their Indian visitors back in 1914 too, and so a wall had to be built around the Pavilion and Dome, partly to protect the Indians from becoming a type of 'zoo' exhibit for curious Brightonians (although locals soon managed to use local double-decker buses to view the soldiers). The wall had a secondary purpose too as it was designed to prevent the soldiers visiting local prostitutes, who were doing a roaring trade in a town full of military men of all types.

Part of the Royal Pavilion & Museums Trust today, Hove Museum is also always worth a visit. It is housed in a beautiful yellow-brick Italianate villa that was built in 1877 for the Vallance family by Thomas Lainson and was originally surrounded by open farmland. It also merits a visit as in the First World War it was a military hospital, before being used to house German prisoners of war and then later being purchased by Hove Council in 1926. If you want to celebrate the city's other military hospitals from the First World War then two other main ones were what is now BHASVIC (Brighton, Hove and Sussex VI Form College), then the boys' grammar school, or the Kitchener Hospital, which is now Brighton General hospital.

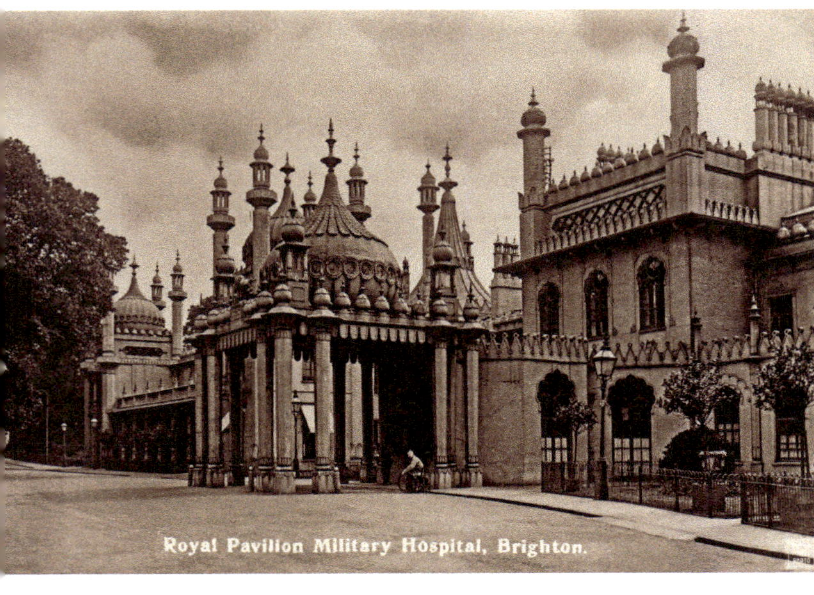

The Royal Pavilion.

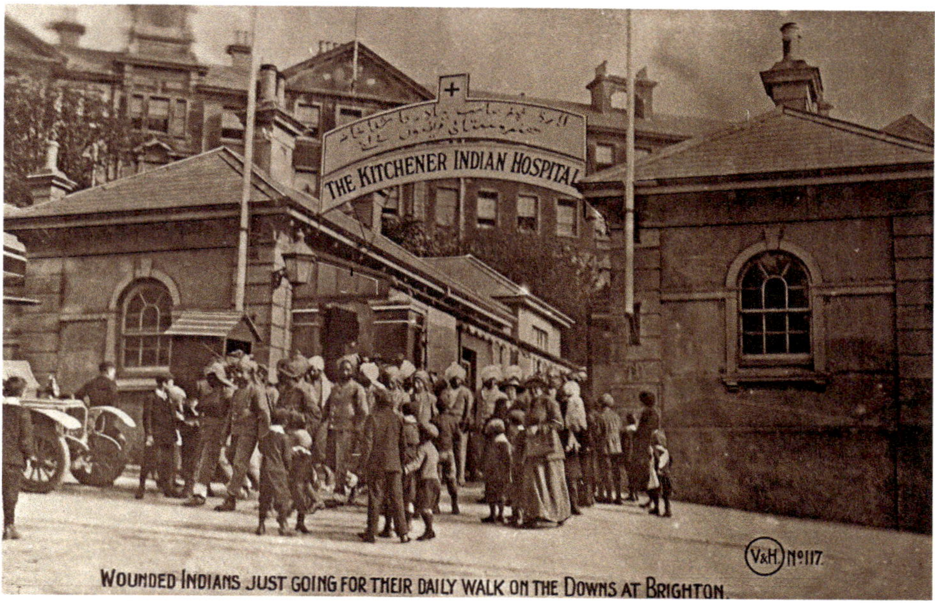

The Kitchener Indian Hospital – one of several military hospitals set up in Brighton during the First World War. This is now Brighton General Hospital.

An adopted Brightonian who merits celebration from this time is American millionaire Alfred Gwynn Vanderbilt I, who brought wealth and fame to the town due to his resurrection of horse-drawn travel to London for the rich and famous. His horse-drawn service, which started at the Metropole, was a great success until thirty of the horses were requisitioned for service in the First World War. Vanderbilt was said to be devastated as he knew all the horses' temperaments well and talked to each of them. This horse whisperer subsequently dedicated his wealth and energy into the war effort and supported the supply of what was a new development – that of motorised ambulances to the Western Front. It was in personally overseeing the transport of these ambulances that he was drowned on 7 May 1915 on board the *Lusitania* when the ship was torpedoed by a German U-boat. His last act was one of chivalrous and gentlemanly behaviour: giving his life jacket to save a female passenger, Miss Annie Middleton. She, unlike this brave and caring man, was one of the few survivors of that famously sad and historic shipping disaster.

The First World War took a major step towards its end in 1918 just outside of Brighton. The decision to cease fighting was taken by Prime Minister Lloyd George and members of his cabinet at Danny House, just outside Hurstpierpoint. Danny House is a residential retirement home today and not generally open to the public, but its main hall was the site of a meeting of the Imperial War Cabinet on 13 October 1918. The terms of the Armistice were agreed here and then cabled to Woodrow Wilson, the American president. In the hall at that time were three future prime ministers – Bonar Law, Balfour and Churchill – and incumbent one Lloyd George who was apparently ill in the White Bedroom. He was still able to sign off the

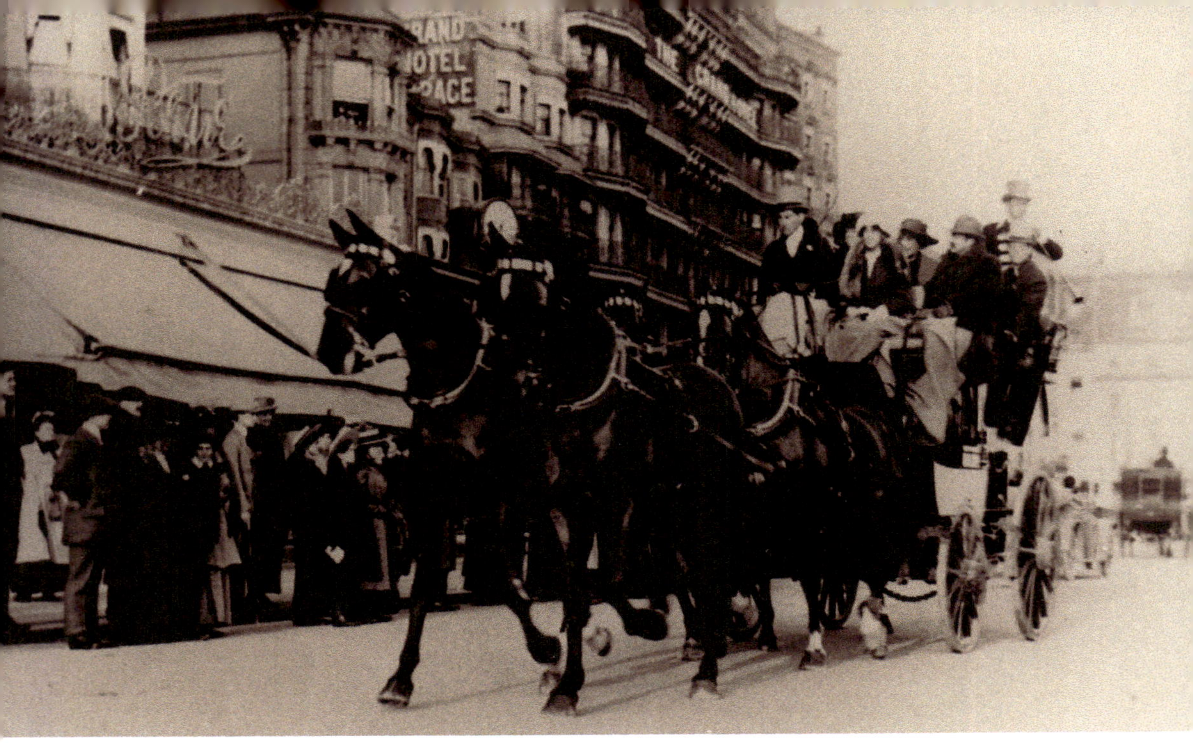

Vanderbilt's coach and horses.

Armistice terms though, and so this local house that had been loaned to Lord Riddell for use by Lloyd George and his cabinet was also able to play a role in the war effort.

Brighton and Hove are not just with linked the end of the war but also the start. Brighton was where the first Allied soldier to fire shots in the First World War was from, and the man who sent the telegram to end the conflict was from Hove. Even when the fighting finished with the Armistice of 11 November 1918, Brighton's association with the end of the war was not yet over. When Lloyd George travelled home after signing the Versailles peace treaty, he walked cheerfully down the gangway when his ship arrived at Folkestone, his wild white hair waving in the breeze and everyone madly cheering the 'Welsh Wizard'. 'Wonderful, wonderful, wonderful!' he said to the Welsh regiment who greeted him. And what was the ship that bought him and the other peacemakers home? A paddle steamer called SS *Brighton*.

Before victory could be achieved morale needed to be kept high, so the Sussex game of stoolball was chosen in 1917 to feature at the wartime-requisitioned County Cricket Ground in Hove. The two teams consisted of a team of elderly lawyers 'damaged by age' and injured soldiers hospitalised at the Royal Pavilion who were 'damaged by wounds'. Despite the wounded servicemen's team having one arm missing each, they still managed to beat the elderly legal eagles. Sport continued to lift spirits in the dark days of the following war, with one such example being a wonderful match between the Royal Australian Airforce servicemen based at the Brighton's Metropole Hotel and local auxiliary firemen. Despite only managing to recruit around a hundred spectators the match was a lively one. The firemen were captained by local Sussex wicketkeeper 'Tich' Cornford and Aussie Flight Sergeant Keith Miller hit a six that shattered the cricket pavilion's clock.

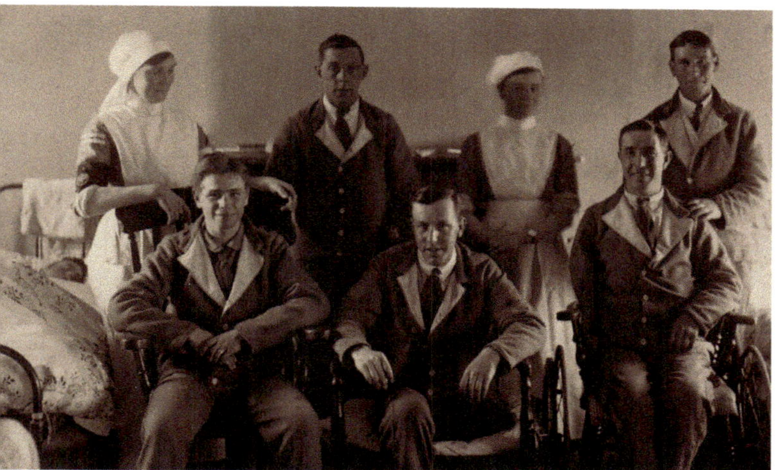

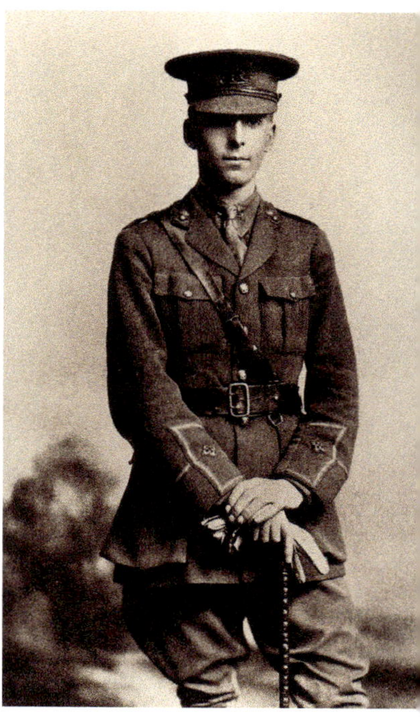

Above: Patients at the Pavilion Hospital for Limbless Men, *c.* 1917.

Right: Second Lieutenant Vere Benett-Stanford.

The war wasn't a game for Sussex's women, who signed up in the Second World War in the armed forces or as spies operating in Nazi-occupied countries. Thankfully, deaths of servicewomen weren't that numerous. To find a grave of one, head just outside of Brighton and Hove to Southwick Cemetery. It has ten Second World War servicepeople buried there; one of them is Joan Horsfall, who died in 1944 in the Women's Auxiliary Air Force.

Despite the horrors of the two world wars, some benefits came as a result of the conflicts and the loss of life they caused. The heir to Preston Manor, Vere Benett-Stanford, didn't survive long after his service in the First World War and with his father's death (who hoped to inherit the house, being cut out of the will by his mother) Preston Manor was given to the people of Brighton. This 'precious national asset' as the *Brighton Herald* once described it can now be enjoyed by all of us, and so from a tragedy Brighton gained a wonderful house and gardens in the north of the city today. Following the war South Moulsecoomb was the first Brighton housing estate to be built. It aimed to be the first example of the 'homes for heroes' promised after the war for ex-servicemen. Just after the war the estate even had a composer living there: William Havergal Brian (1896–1972), who composed 'Gothic Symphony', which, as it needed 200 musicians to play, was the biggest symphony ever written at that time.

Heading west, Portslade is an overlooked part of Brighton and Hove but was once bigger than Hove, and the village part is always worth an explore – north of the Old Shoreham Road. Once known as Copperas Gap, the south end was also important as a bustling port, which is now part of Shoreham Harbour. The busy

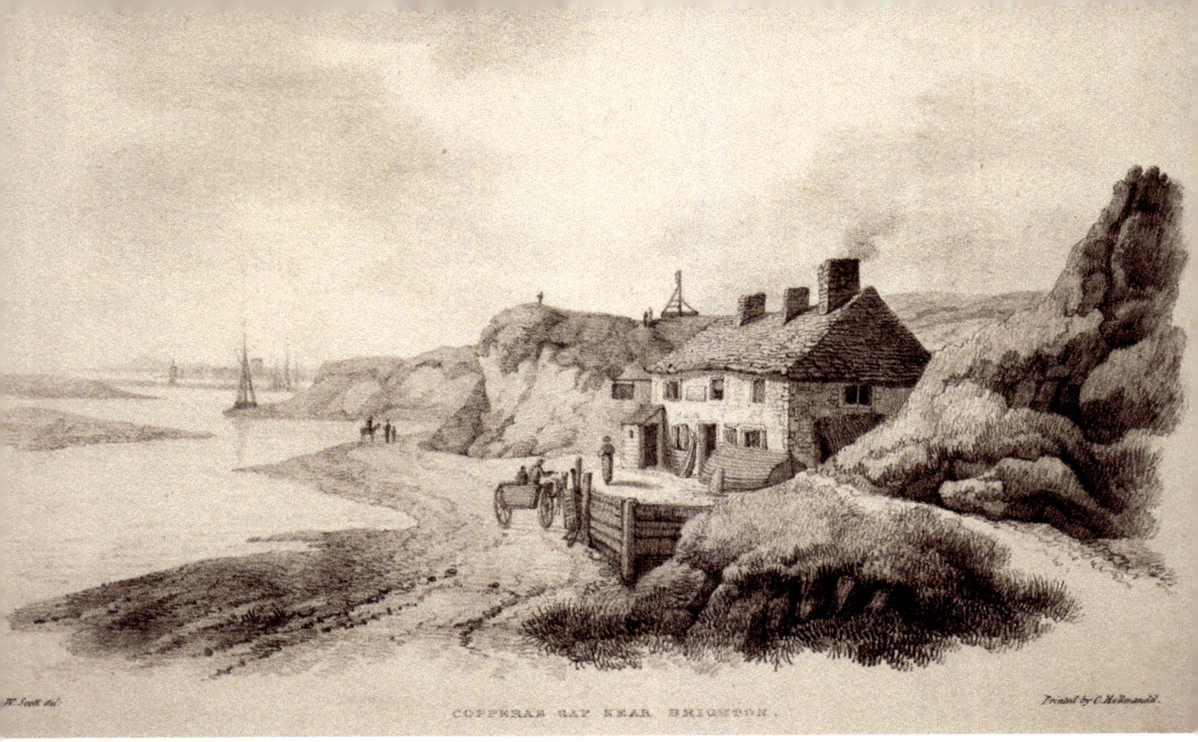

Copperas Gap – today the Portslade part of Shoreham Harbour.

south part of Portslade needed its own police station, which it got in St Andrew's Road in 1908. Today this old police station is unique as it was mothballed in the 1950s and, although empty, still has many of its original Edwardian features, including three of the original Edwardian police cells intact at the rear. Behind these cells is something even rarer, however, that not many people have ever seen. As Portslade was such a vital port (Shoreham is the nearest coastal port to London) it became a decontamination centre at the start of the Cold War in the 1940s. This was because if the Russians used chemical or biological weapons, soldiers or civilians could be treated for the effects. As the Russians developed

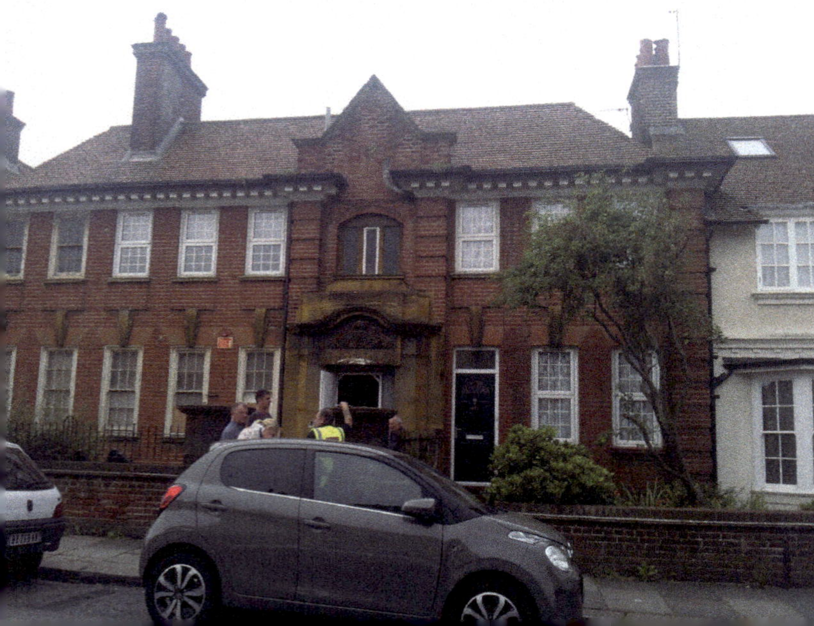

The front of Portslade Old Police Station.

nuclear weapons this bunker at the back of the police station became a nuclear decontamination centre – one of only six in the UK. Radiation-exposed VIPs or key people would have passed through its shower room if they survived a nuclear blast or contamination. The block still exists today. Thankfully, it was never used, except when the local bobbies decided to help the odd drunk cool off, but Portslade still has this remarkable and rare legacy of the Cold War in a residential street.

At this point I would like to encourage the readers of this book and residents of Brighton and Hove (well, quite frankly, anywhere) to adopt a new annual tradition to celebrate our wartime heroes. I will also start this with an admission that may sound quite strange to some. I love cemeteries. Choosing to spend a chunk of your day with the dead sounds a bit weird (but then if you've ever met half of my friends then you'll know spending time with the alive can be much stranger). Cemeteries with no church attached are the forgotten bits of our towns, villages and cities. We don't venture into them much due to decades of exposure to scary movies, but I want to argue that Armistice Sunday is the time to embrace these neglected, fascinating, and even beautiful bits of our county every November.

The nearest Sunday to 11 November each year is usually Armistice Sunday, and it is the day I suggest Brighton and Hove should embrace 'Cemetery Sunday' each year. Now please don't get me wrong, I'm not suggesting we ignore the important ceremonies that many attend at our war memorials. What I am saying is that we need to add to what we already have, not take away or have a competition to see who can commemorate the best. We should have a whole day of not just remembering our war dead but thanking them too for the gift we were given – our freedom and the lives we lead today.

Sacrifices of the past mean we can and should look to the future. With the centenary of the Armistice recently and the centenary of the first ever Armistice Commemorations of 1919 just gone, is it not time to reassess what we should and could do at this time of year? When you read the accounts of the demobbed soldiers of 1919 in books such as Max Arthur's fantastic *The Road Home*, you realise not all soldiers agreed on how the day should be spent. Some wanted to be remembered, some wanted public change. Some merely wanted to be left alone and to remember the dead with those who survived alongside them from the trenches. There was disagreement over the purpose of the day even then. Perhaps it is time for us to reassess its role, especially at this time, a century on, when our country is still fractured and divided over its future. Jo Cox MP famously said, 'We are far more united and have far more in common with each other than things that divide us.' We need a day where we come together through one of the things we have in common and that, no matter our colour, class or background, is remembrance of loved ones and gratitude for those who fought for us.

Brighton and Hove is certainly an inclusive city so for some we have to realise that attending memorial services just isn't possible and we do need to explore alternatives. This is where our cemeteries come in. On Cemetery Sunday each year, either before, after or instead of attending a Remembrance service, grab yourself a map, your GPS on your phone, some tracing paper and pencils for the little 'uns, a few poppies and head to the cemeteries that contain our war dead. You will be going to the places where some of the people who fought for us and died for us actually are, not just the place where our war dead are remembered.

Cemeteries are theme parks. I mean no disrespect by that. I have taken, and still take, numerous visitors to cemeteries here and on the Western Front every year and always insist on respect for those buried there, but there are numerous myths about these places that need dispersing. You do not need to be silent in a cemetery and they are certainly not places you should be miserable in. Those buried below the grass would not want you to be. Rather than Paulton's Park or Chessington, visit Bear Road, Woodvale, Hove or Portslade Cemetery instead. The 'theme' here is learning, remembrance and investigating the past. And these are still definitely parks. They are free, open to the public, and provide green spaces. What is great about them, as my friend and fellow tour guide Amanda Jane Scales says, is 'they are a time capsule of the past, full of fascinating stories'.

Like all good providers of stories they leave you asking questions and wanting to find out more. How did they die? What was happening in the year their life ended on the tombstone? What is an 'MM'? Why are the servicemen all mostly buried in rows facing the same way? Why do the tombstones all look nearly the same? Why do they all have plants in front of them? Why have they got poppies on them? Amanda and I both love taking people to cemeteries, and for me taking my own children is a great time to spend time with them as they ask these questions and it makes them want to discover more, especially if like us you have a relative buried in one of them. Tracing paper and pencils let you take grave rubbings of battalion badges, messages relatives paid for on the graves and make interesting collages at home or support lessons at school. For my boys, having their great-great grandfather buried in Bear Road Cemetery makes them ask questions about themselves, their Nanny and me. The answers can be scary. Had my great-grandfather died a year before from his lung problems or not made it through the war as a machine gunner, then my grandad would not be here and neither would they. Stuff like this is powerful and makes you appreciate that we need to know about these events more than we realise. History is not just events in books, it is me and them.

Brighton and Hove is a city of hills and many other Sussex cemeteries and graveyards are likewise on hills or in beautiful places. Bear Road and Woodvale both provide spectacular views down over Brighton, which not enough people see. You can park for free and explore – see if you can find the German Airforce graves in Bear Road. What you won't avoid is exercise and fresh air – how ironic that places of the dead are places that are good for your health. If you head out of the city to graveyards such as Duncton Chapel in Wiston you are near Roman building materials and a view looking up at Chanctonbury Ring.

For those outside of Brighton and Hove who don't dwell in what was a 'hospital town', war graves can be found in the most unusual locations. Even the Sussex

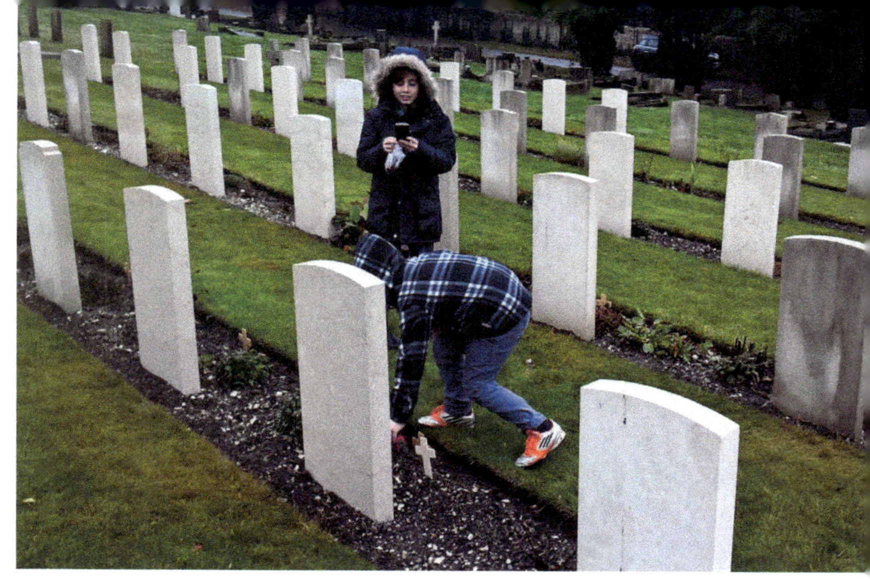

village of Washington has a tiny cemetery with a war grave of a Home Guard who died on duty in the Second World War, now forever looking up at the beautiful chalk pits above the village. Does it even matter if there are no war graves in your local cemetery or graveyard? Of course not. Looking for the white Portland stone rectangular war graves is part of the challenge. You will still find names on civilian tombs that you may remember. This was the way the original creators of *EastEnders* found the names for the first families of that soap. You can investigate further with the Commonwealth War Graves site: www.cwgc.org.

So, for views, peace, solitude, a history lesson, kinaesthetic learning, art, stories, health and adventure, embrace 'Cemetery Sunday' every November, and if you're not attending a memorial service make this family adventure or walk with friends part of your annual calendar. Follow it up with a good family meal afterwards and maybe an old war film or book and you have the recipe for a truly British Thanksgiving.

A view of Brighton from Woodvale Cemetery.

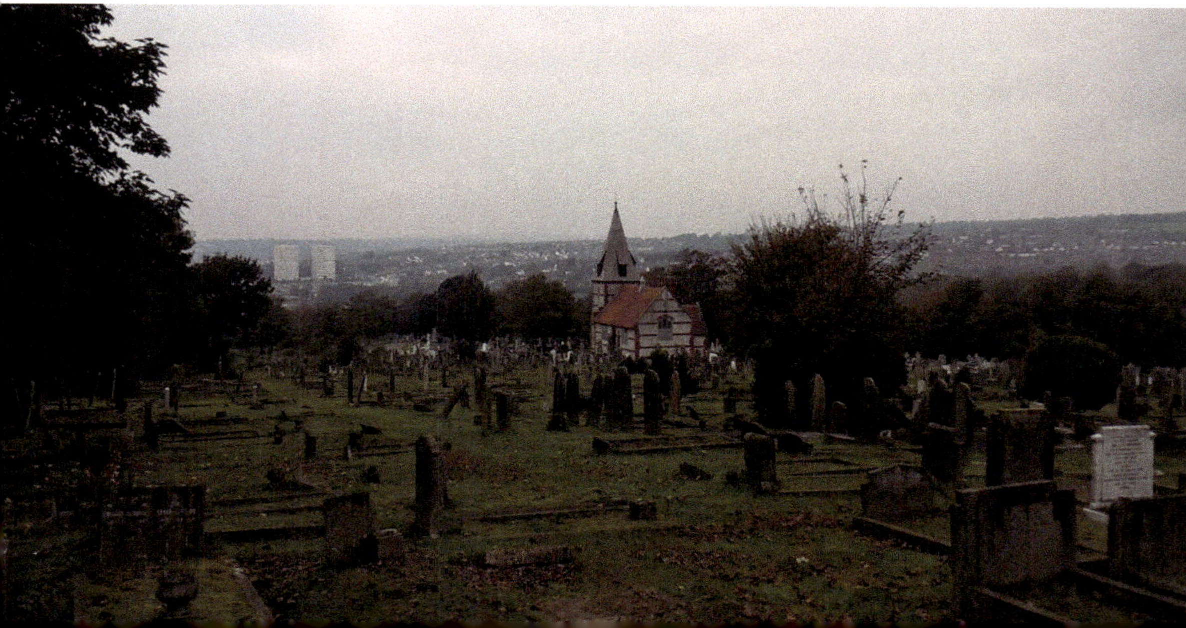

Famous For and Firsts

In this chapter we celebrate areas where Brighton and Hove have led, such as health, holidaymaking, industry, film and photography. We explore what truly makes Brighton Brighton and what the city is known for around the world.

We shall start with food. The mangle-wurzel, a type of root vegetable related to beetroot and mostly used for feeding livestock, was first introduced to England by Thomas Pelling, vicar of Ovingdean. Numerous British animals have thrived on this crop, especially dairy animals. It has provided a number of cultural references (spelt differently), giving us the 1970s West Country band The Wurzels and *Wurzel Gummidge* – the show about a loveable scarecrow, which was back on the with a revival at Christmas 2019. The vegetable soon grew in popularity, and in south Somerset, Norfolk and Wales during Punkie Night (celebrated on the last Thursday of October), children carry around lanterns called 'Punkies', which are hollowed out mangle-wurzels. The root has also been used for mangold hurling – a sport that dates back to the eleventh century, where participants stand inside a wicker basket and hurl the root as far as they can. The root can also be used to brew a potent alcoholic beverage. If you wish to grow and eat them seeds can be hard to find, but you are advised to eat them when small as when larger they are better for animals. Should you therefore wish to celebrate the great farming Brighton hero that is Thomas Pelling then both he and his import are mentioned on his gravestone at Ovingdean Church graveyard.

Houses though, rather than horticulture is where Brighton boasts its greatest number of firsts. Marlborough House was built in 1769 and, in its first incarnation, was the first house on the Steine. It was purchased by the Duke of Marlborough, who bought it in 1771. It was then purchased by MP William Hamilton in 1788 and transformed by the architect Robert Adam to its current, stucco-covered state. This meant that Hamilton and Prince George competed at this time in Brighton's history to see who had the town's most splendid house. Not many houses can be said to have competed with a royal palace-to-be! One last fact is that there was more than one Marlborough House in Brighton. The duke moved in 1778 to Grove House, where the Pavilion's music room is today, and this house also took the duke's name. This red-brick building was demolished as the Pavilion expanded, so today we just have the one – rather wonderful –

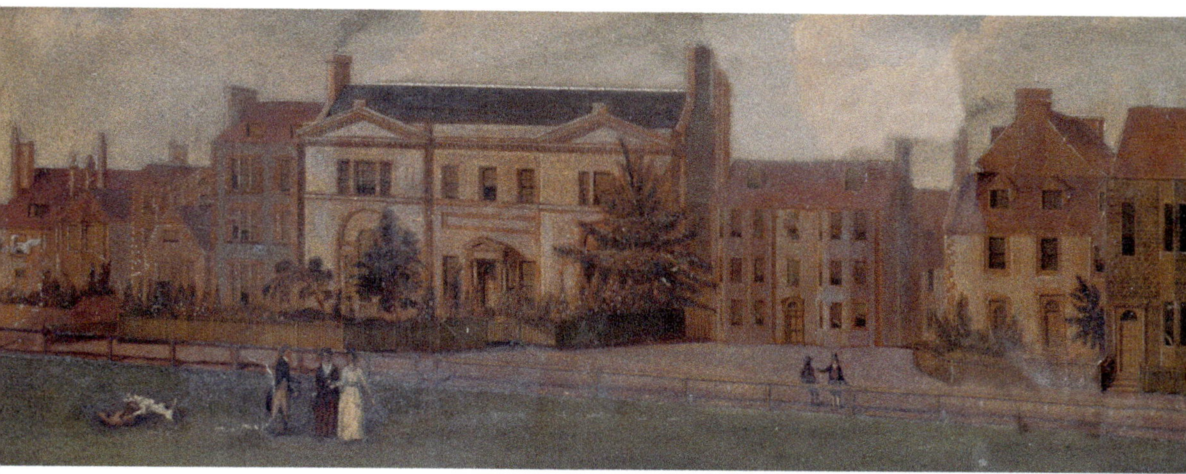

Marlborough House. The idea of illustrious buildings embracing sea views came slightly later. Royal Crescent, built between 1798 and 1807 on the East Cliffs and fronted with black 'mathematical' tiles, was the first crescent of houses to be built deliberately facing the sea.

The Georgian and Victorian ages saw Brighton chalk up a wealth of other firsts. Its Chain Pier was not the first pier (it was in fact the third), but it was the first to be widely celebrated, as well as being arguably the world's first pleasure pier. The West Pier today (despite its skeletal frame being all that remains from the 1866 pier) is a Grade I listed building. The Grand was one of the first hotels in the world to have electric light throughout when it opened in 1866, and Magnus Volk, whose own house was the first to be lit by electricity in the town, was also responsible for lighting the Royal Pavilion with electricity in 1884. Brighton's aquarium (today the Sea Life Centre) is the world's oldest operating aquarium. It opened on 10 August 1872 at a cost of £133,000 (in today's money around £5.5 million). Ninety-nine years after the aquarium opened, on 20 August 1971 it was listed as a Grade II building. Although the building has seen many changes, the magnificent main hall has survived with tanks either side. It is constructed with a vaulted-brick ceiling supported by polished granite or stone columns that are decorated with carved stone marine capitals in a Victorian Gothic style.

The original design was meant to have towers and turrets, but these weren't built as it was felt they would spoil sea views. Preston Park may not have sea views, being 3 miles north of the sea, but it is Brighton's biggest ornamental park and it includes Britain's oldest velodrome in the north-east corner, which opened in 1877. In 1896 Brighton was important in another type of movement as it was the first place outside the capital to show moving film – in the same year. In religious buildings we led the way as our synagogue in Middle Street was the first in the country to have electric light when consecrated in 1875.

The Brighton Metropole was opened fifteen years later in 1890. It had the country's first heated staircase, which was powered by steam and seen as incredibly

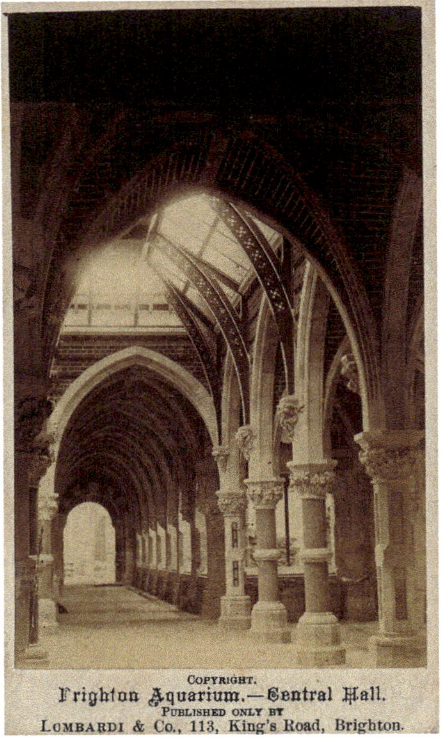

Left and below: Brighton Aquarium.

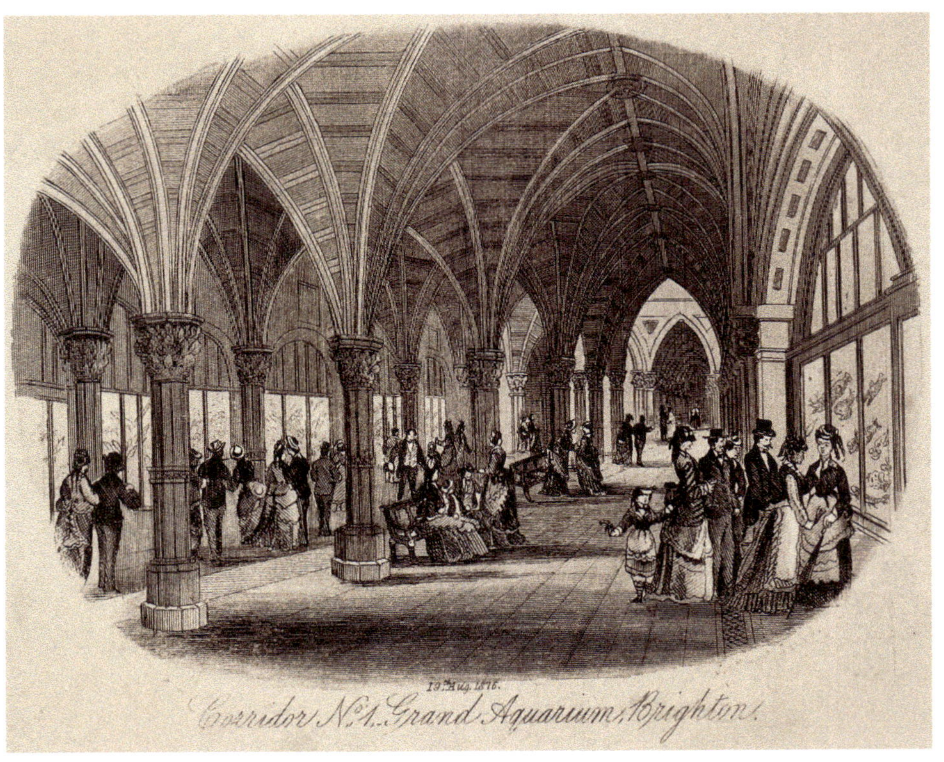

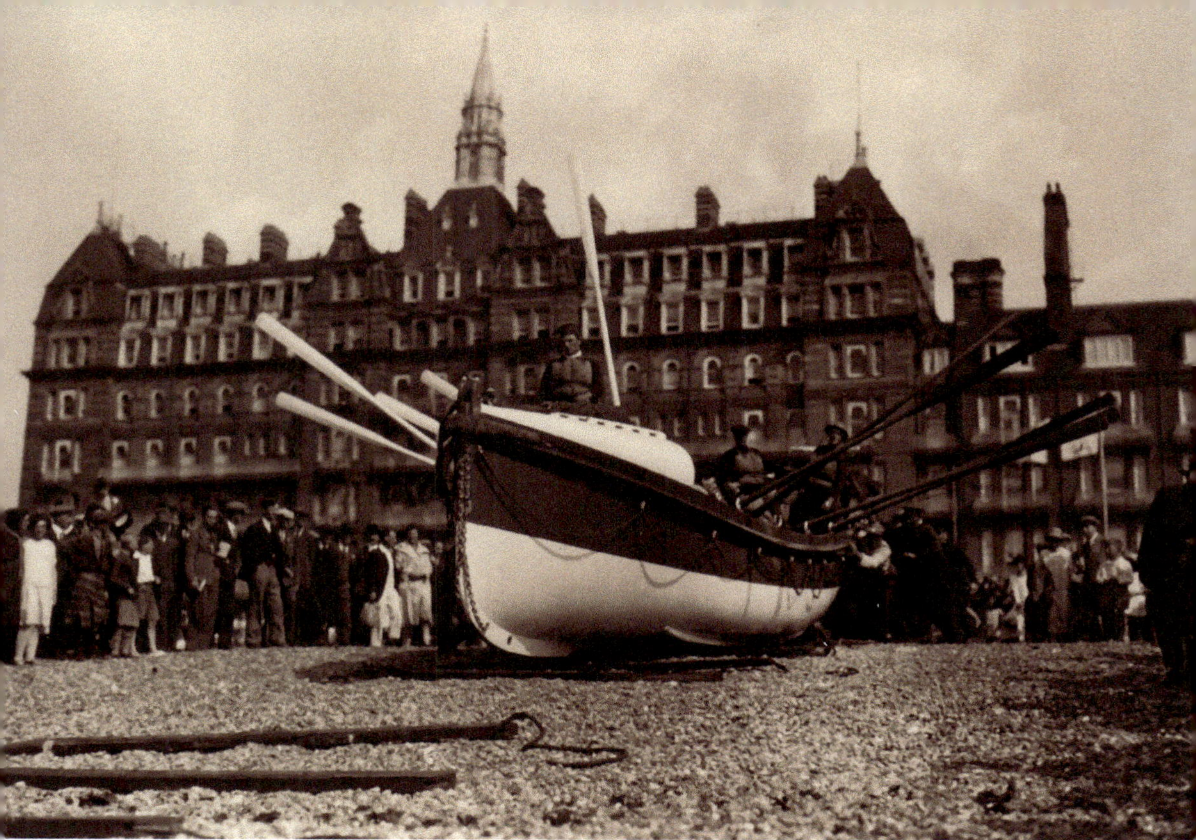

luxurious at the time. The Metropole cost a massive £57,000 to build in 1890, and its size meant Brighton became the location of the nation's largest hotel outside the capital. Royalty, the aristocracy, and the internationally rich and famous all flocked to Brighton, willing to pay the £3 8s a day for the luxurious suites that offered hot and cold tap and seawater to guests. It was the first British hotel to have the exclusive name 'Metropole' after Cannes and Monte Carlo outside of London. The hotel was also important in early motoring as Brighton's first visit by a motor car ended up at the Metropole in 1896, and the world-famous London to Brighton car race, which still runs today, originally ended at the hotel then too.

The Old Ship Hotel has also been involved in many firsts throughout its long history. The hotel has been a courthouse, housed a post office before the Town Hall existed, it has been a coaching inn, and has also hosted an auction house. It was where the idea of a veteran car club that would create Brighton's annual Veteran Car Run was first mooted. A century later, it also moved with the times, where as early as 1996 it was the first in the town to give all its guests internet access and their own email account. This following account from the *Argus* in February 1996 was exciting news twenty years ago: 'The hotel has its own pages on the World Wide Web. Prospective guests can now access directions to the hotel, look at a typical bedroom, find out what facilities are available, or even learn something of the hotel's history.'

Brighton doesn't just have historic hotels, it also has one of the UK's oldest cinemas. The Duke of York's Picturehouse opened in Brighton in 1910, so it is not

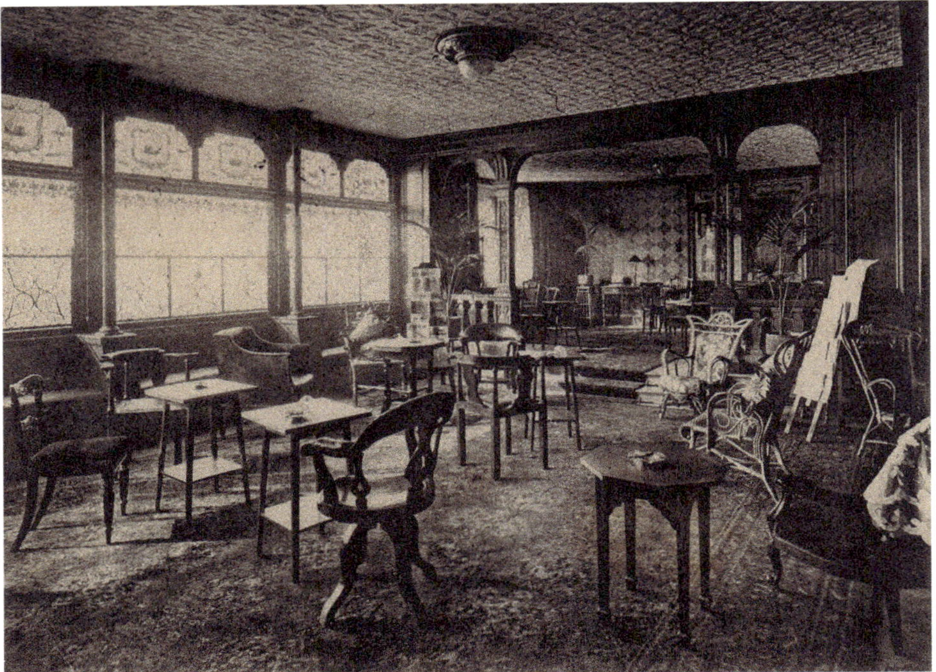

The lounge of the Old Ship Hotel.

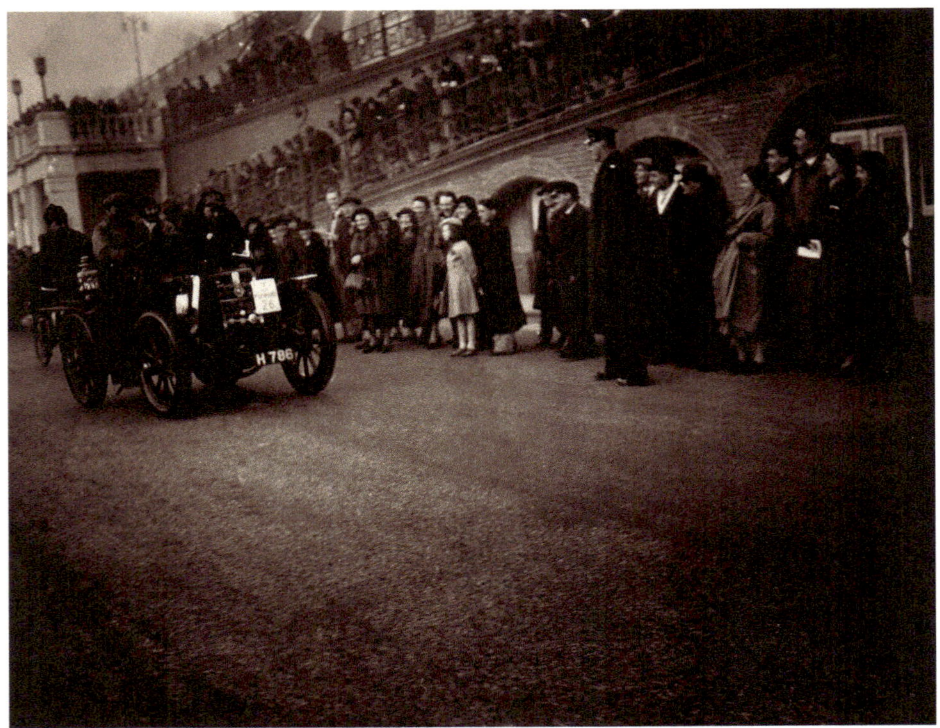

The Veteran Car Race as a car approaches the finish line on Madeira Drive.

surprising that the earliest developments in cinema and films also took place here. William Freise-Greene, early cinematography pioneer, carried out a number of his experiments in Brighton. Brighton, around 1900, is where the modern movie was created – years before Hollywood was up and running. The long hours of summer sunlight, lack of London smog and fresh air attracted a group of people in this new experimental industry to Brighton and nearby Shoreham: film makers. The group, led by George Albert Smith, who'd been a Brighton impresario of traditional theatre shows, even invented the technique of the first ever close-up shot in his experimentation. They started the bold new move – at this time – of *moving* the camera. Brighton and Sussex have remained ever since a popular location for film making.

Clarendon Mansions in Hove was designed and lived in by the father of Frederick William Lanchester (1868–1946), the name behind early British car company Lanchester. They were the first British car company to use a petrol engine and also created the first petrol-powered bus in the UK. Brighton was also the destination for the country's first planned motorway, but this never reached fruition.

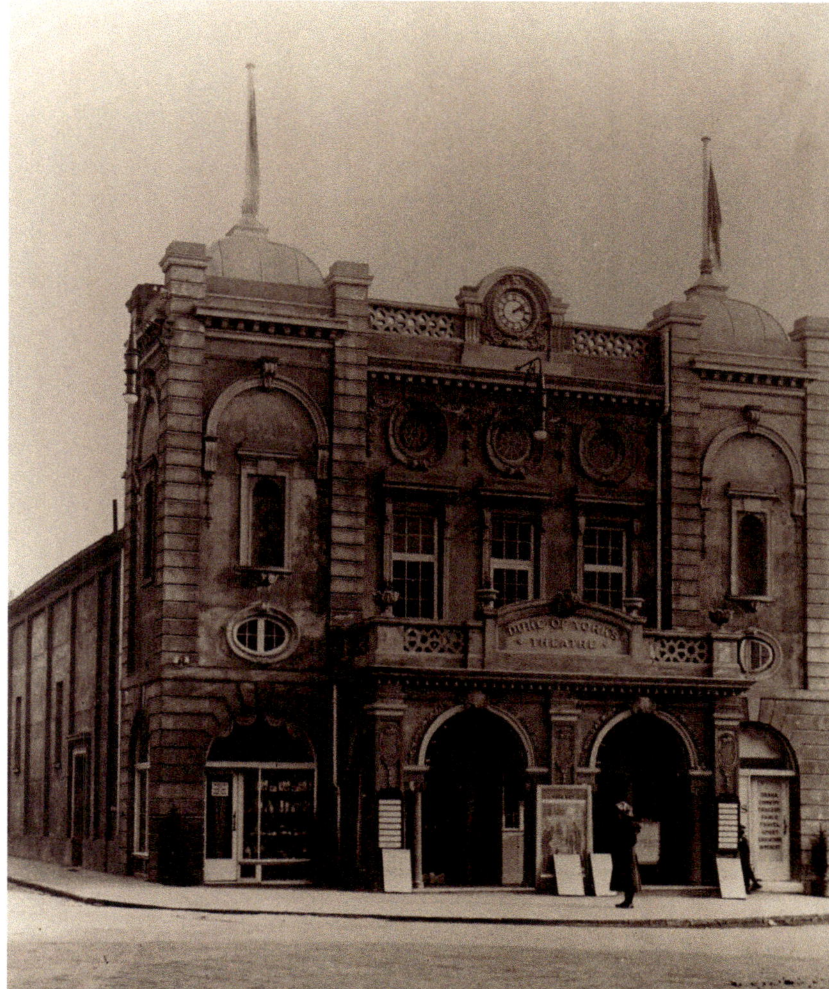

The Duke of York's Theatre.

Brighton's hotels helped the town become a dedicated conference and exhibition venue, which brought much needed revenue to a town deserted by holidaymakers and looking decidedly past its best. Exhibitions also brought a range of 'firsts' to Brighton. The first ever Disc Festival (in other words a record and music fair) took place in the town in August 1962. Britain's first-ever Fast-food Fair soon followed, as well as the country's first exhibition of its kind for the greetings card industry. Technology meant the Brighton could even hold events organised from the US, and delegates and exhibitors in the Metropole's exhibition halls (pictured) even got to travel up and down Brighton's first escalators. New exhibition halls from the 1960s meant the introduction of new or unusual features for the time, such as air conditioning, CCTV, Brighton's first escalator and intriguingly at the Metropole, according to one flyer, 'a floor surface that is not tiring'. From 1961 the Metropole had the country's first licensed casino and also the Starlit Room, which was the first rooftop restaurant in the country – it was built on top of the Metropole. This restaurant, at 150 feet high, was the place to be for several royals and numerous VIPs during the 1970s; today it is called the Chartwell Suite. The Metropole boasts one other first: Kylie Minogue played her first ever live performance in Britain at the Metropole in the late 1980s.

The Brighton Centre opened in September 1977 and shortly before this Hove Town hall was the first new town hall to be built in Britain after the war. Unfortunately, within months after its completion in 1974, cracks were developing in the concrete structure. By 1978, contractors were brought back in to repair cracks. By the 1980s there was no longer enough room for all the staff so the building had to be developed further; the new block was hugely hot in the summer (111 degrees Fahrenheit was recorded in 1989) and staff froze in winter. This then cost a further £16,500 to sort, but by 1990 the building was still seen as too small and another £380,000 was spent increasing the size of the Town Hall further. Perhaps Hove should have just repaired the original beautiful Alfred Waterhouse-designed Victorian town hall that existed before it and expanded that as needed. The name Hove Town Hall now has been officially discontinued since 2001. It is now just the Hove Centre.

Despite the world-famous international Winkle Club being founded in Hastings, it was rival Brighton that held the world's first ever Winkle Picking Championships in July 1989 on the Palace Pier. Under the sharp eye of TV commentator Alan Weeks, fifteen teams of winkle-pickers fought to win the world title by extracting as many winkles as they could in just two minutes. Watching holidaymakers could also buy packs of winkles to eat for £1 and help raise funds for the NSPCC. The winners were the Bedford Hotel (today the Holiday Inn) who beat Brighton's police, fire brigade, Concorde nightclub, traffic wardens and (best of all) fishmongers by removing 124 winkles from shells to win the title of world's fastest winkle-pickers. For their troubles they were awarded a coveted silver platter – thankfully without any more winkles on it. Brighton's police

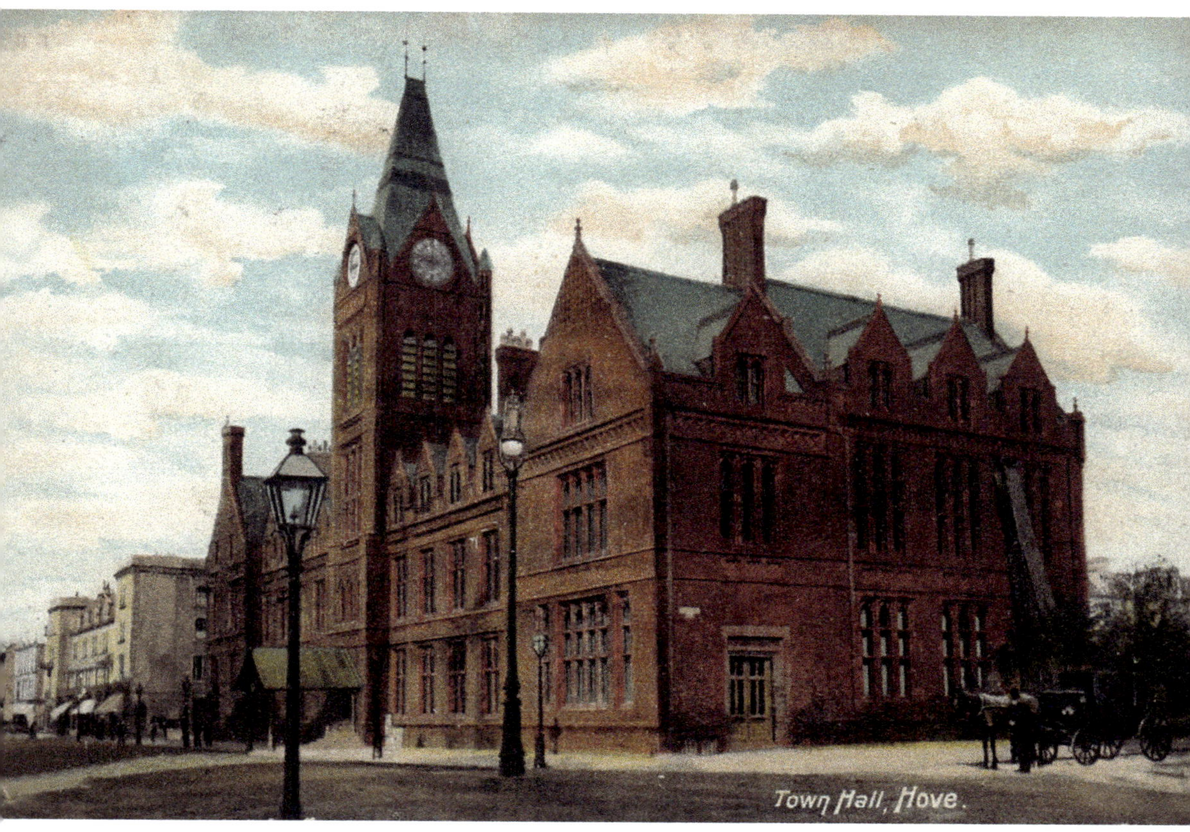

The original Hove Town Hall, 1904.

shouldn't have been too worried about this defeat as they had other firsts to their credit. They were the first in the country to use personal radios. We can even credit Brighton Police for the look of *Doctor Who*'s TARDIS, as our bobbies were the first force to introduce the famous blue police boxes.

Back in 1991 the *Argus* reported on Brighton's first female publican, Barbara White, who was landlady of the Duke of Wellington for nearly twenty-five years. Neighbouring Hove boasted not one but two leading lady licensees: publicans Linda and Pauline Diamond – a year later in 1992 her daughter managed to gain the first ever full licence for an outdoor bar. The mother and daughter team, christened the 'Double Diamonds' by the *Argus* after a type of beer at that time, took over the Stadium pub in Hove (today a Co-op store) and asked magistrates for a beer garden with its own licensed bar. To ensure parents inside could keep an eye on their children in the garden bar, Linda and Pauline discovered that the wall legally needed to separate the bars could be only a cheeky 1 foot high. The pub was also staffed entirely by women – something unusual at that time, even unbelievably as recently as the 1990s. Double Diamond beer is still apparently brewed in small quantities today as it is Prince Phillip's favourite ale, according to a book by royal butler Paul Burrell.

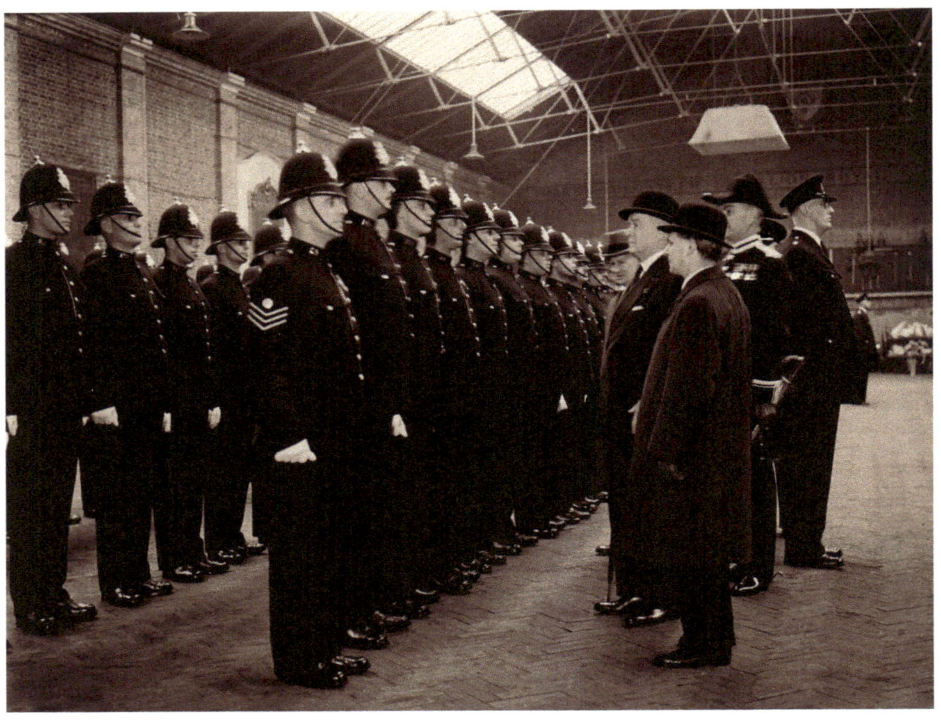

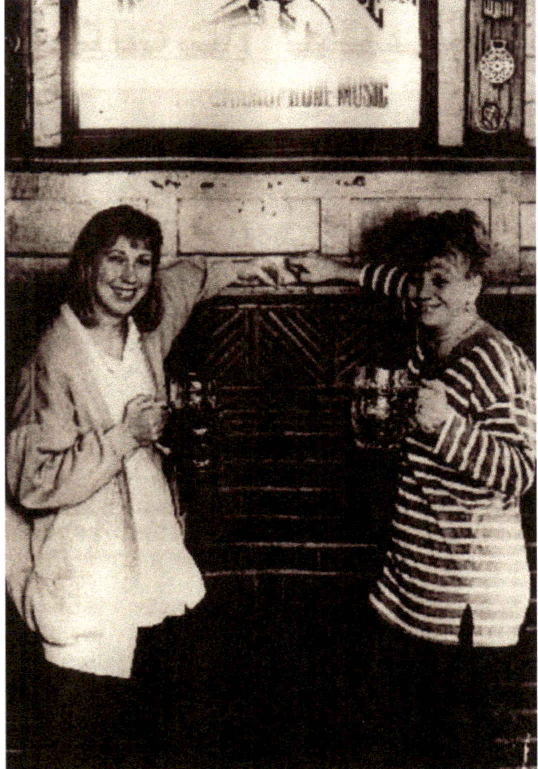

Above: Brighton's police.

Left: The 'Double Diamonds'.
(*The Argus*)

Health and Wealth

Brighton was recently voted the most popular British seaside destination on a list of thirty locations people considered 'happy places'. Below Brighton was Padstow in Cornwall, which was chosen by 17 per cent as their favourite place; the sandy beaches of the Hebrides had 17 per cent; St Ives, also Cornwall, scored 15 per cent; Blackpool Sands had 7 per cent; and Fistral Beach in Newquay had 5 per cent of the vote. *The Argus* recently reported how Brighton was found to be a favourite destination among women in particular, with 23 per cent of those surveyed picking it as one of their happy places compared to 14 per cent of men. It was also popular with sixteen to twenty-four year olds, with more than one in five (the highest number for any age category) enjoying a trip to Brighton for their holidays this year. Organisers of the research said, 'In terms of culture, history and picturesque scenery, many popular European resorts could not compete with the city.' More than one in ten people from Brighton said it also was their favourite holiday location, which suggests how much people love living in the seaside city – Brightonians even feel on holiday in the place they live in!

In his guide to the city in 1761 (Brighton's first ever guidebook), Dr Anthony Relhan suggested that Brighton was a healthy place to come because a lack of trees meant a lack of moisture in the air. Brighton may not have had much moisture from trees (although maybe the sea added slightly to the moisture in the air), but it did have fish. Fish bring us health, and the wealthier you were the more fish you could consume in Regency-era Brighton, and the early nineteenth century was certainly known for its gluttony and huge numbers of courses. Therefore, it's not surprising that the consumer of the biggest fish ever at that time was the Porky Prince himself, George the Prince Regent. The country's biggest ever trout was caught at Bolney during the years that George IV holidayed in Brighton and was indeed given to Porky Prinny to consume. The trout weighed an incredible 22 lbs.

Brighton has been known for centuries for the medicinal properties of its seawater as well as its fish. But did you know we also have chalybeate springs from where water bubbles up to the surface, which were said to cure the sick? St Anne's Well Gardens in Hove was discovered to have a chalybeate spring whose mineral properties helped Brighton grow as a resort for health. The other side of

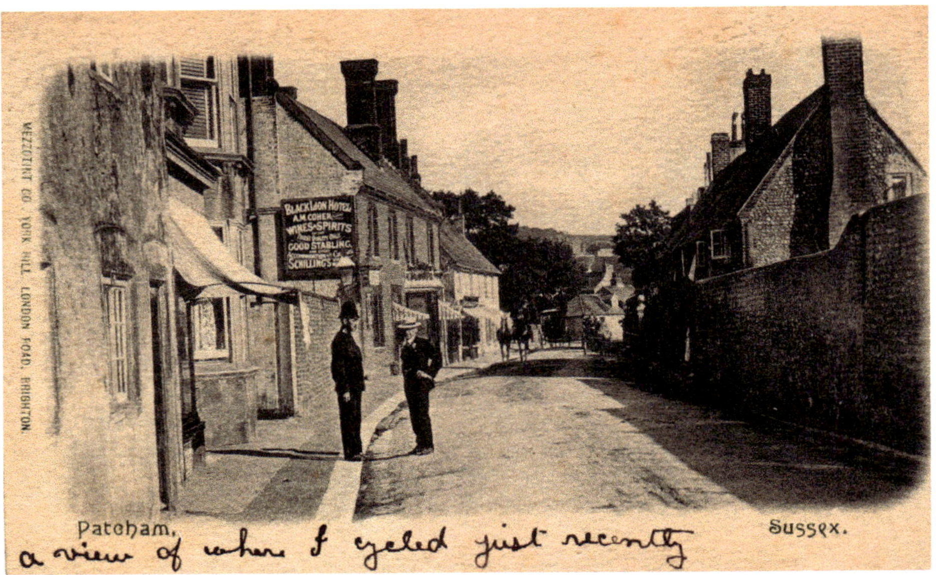

Patcham.

the Downs, Ditchling, also had one that was famed for helping Sussex folk fight rheumatism and other ailments. The spring was famous in the 1800s but had gone out of fashion by the twentieth century. You can still see spring water emerging fresh from under the chalky Downs at Fulking, by the wonderful Shepherd and Dog pub. Brighton's very own hidden river starts under the Downs at Patcham and is 'born' by a well (underground water), hence its name 'Wellesbourne'. Icy spring water also trickles out from under the beach at Brighton that you can spot east of the Palace Pier.

West of the spring water, the Queens Hotel is one of Brighton's most amazing locations. Not only was the site right next to the sea but was also home to Mahomed's Vapour Baths. At a time when slavery was still legal and racial atrocities were taking place across the world, one of Brighton's leading businessmen was Indian. Starting his career as a doctor treating British soldiers in the Raj, Mahomed made his way to Brighton via Ireland where he married an Irishwoman and, aware of the racist attitudes at the time, started treating the wealthy and royal for free. The free samples of his exciting new health treatments included Turkish and vapour baths, and being massaged through a sheet caught on. He soon boasted mounted crutches around his treatment rooms of all the patients he had 'cured'. His fame grew and he was appointed 'Royal Shampooing Surgeon' to both George IV and William IV, gaining him numerous wealthy clients. His technique of massaging using the fingers is what we do today when applying shampoo. Interestingly, this is where the phrase originates: 'shampooing' is an Indian term that has changed its meaning over time. Mahomed lived to the ripe old age of 102 and is buried in St Nicholas's Churchyard today. He deserves celebration as the first Indian to write a book in English and as a businessman

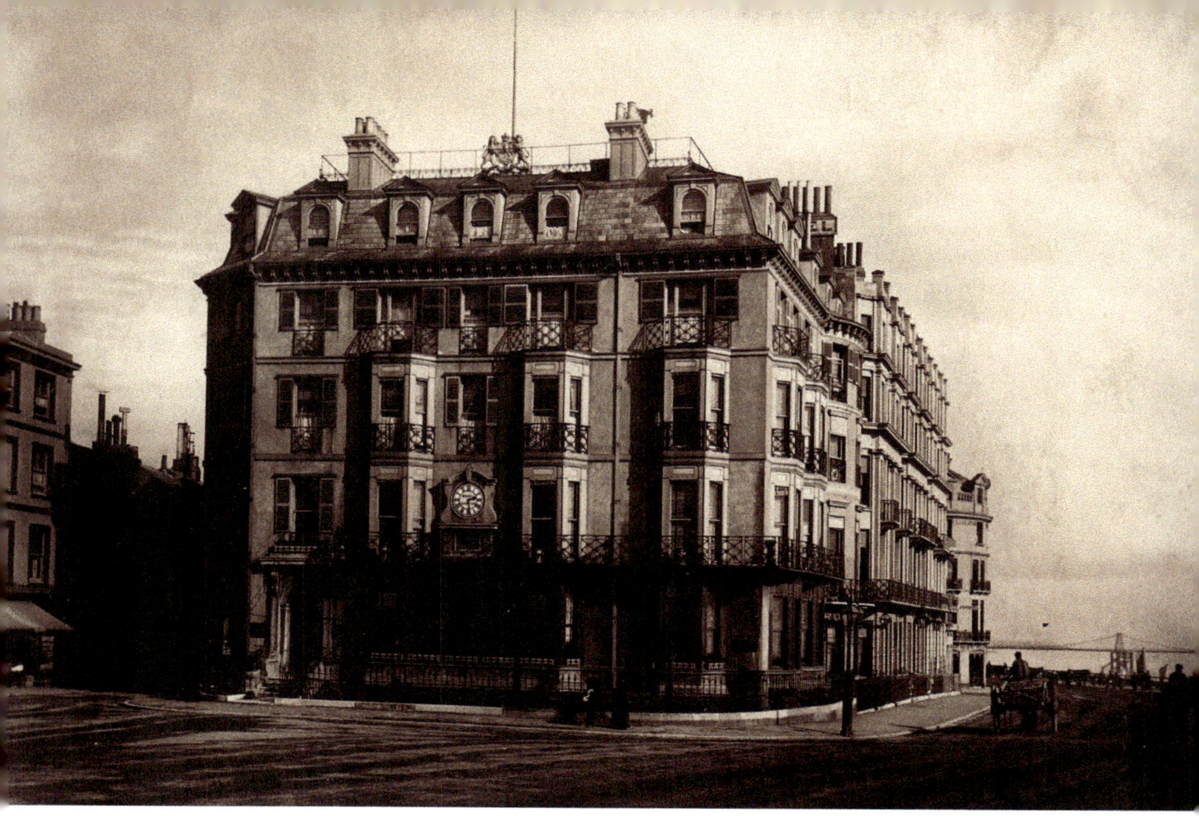

who helped increase the fame and prosperity of Brighton. He also brought Turkish
baths to Britain and introduced the only word with 'poo' in it to the English
language that makes you think of pleasant smells.

As well as Mahomed helping people's health, Brighton's famous adopted doctor
Richard Russell and his successors brought the wealthy of the eighteenth and
early nineteenth centuries to the town for sea cures. Unlike Mahomed, though,

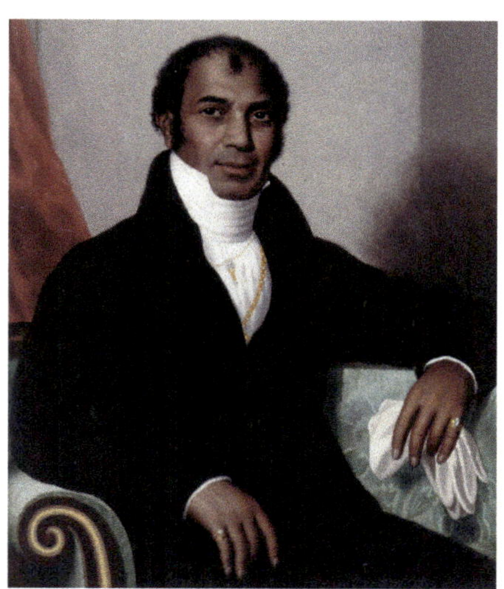

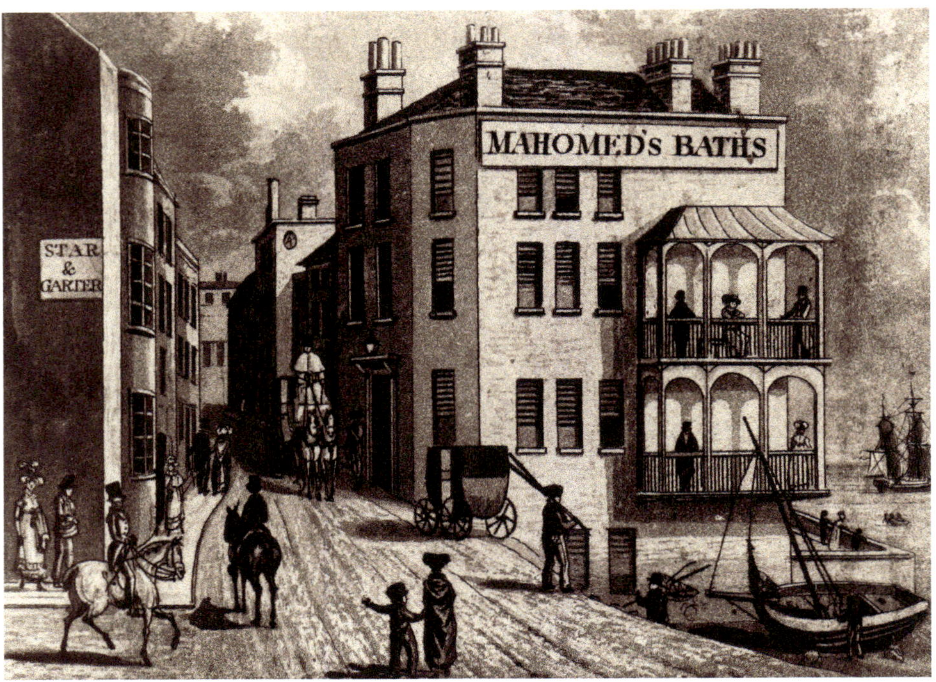

Mahomed's Baths, Brighton.

they prescribed woodlice, crabs' eyes, burnt sponge, cuttlefish bones, vipers' flesh and seawater. Mice were, believe it or not, used in the remoter parts of the county as remedies in the days before pharmacies. It was recommended that you roasted and ate them or crumbled them into a drink. This usage led to a mishearing by one Portslade mother. Her doctor had told her to put some ice in a bag and then hold it on the head of her poorly son, Tommy, to treat a malady. When the good doctor enquired a day later how Tommy was doing, his mum replied that he was feeling much better. 'But Doctor,' she said, 'I'm sorry to say the mice in the bag all died.'

Back in the 1880s, Brighton College perhaps suffered from students imbibing for 'medicinal purposes kindly allowed hampers to occasionally be sent from home, but stated firmly that 'They must not contain wine.' Allowing alcohol wasn't a problem, it seems, in the college's earliest years though, as from 1845 until the 1870s boys were allowed a pint of ale with lunch and another with dinner. This was halved in 1876 and ended up in 1885 applying only to the senior boys, but it might explain the two-hour lunchbreaks they had! Beer, of course, at this time was traditionally drunk by children as it had been purified through brewing, whereas water and milk were still often seen as dangerous.

To no doubt improve their health Brighton taxi driver Kenneth Butler and his wife Edith swapped asking for a fare for welfare when they moved to a warmer climate. They were able to do this when in 1986, after thirty years, they sold their Brighton taxi firms and opened a café-bar in Majorca. They decided to take a bit of Brighton with them, though, calling their venue in Torenova the Brighton Belle.

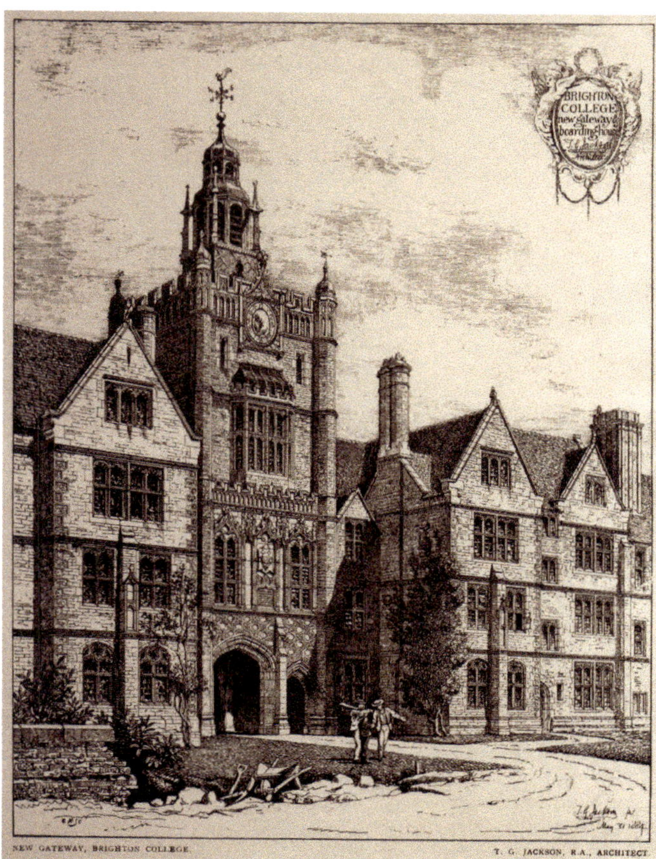

Right: New Gateway, Brighton College.

Below: The Butlers. (*The Argus*)

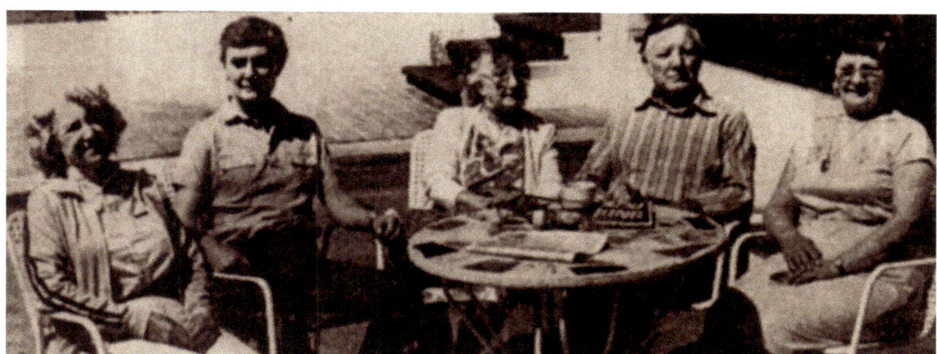

Their major benefit was apparently the cheap price of alcohol, with beer then at 58p a pint and a triple brandy at 45p. 'You don't measure, you just pour,' Mr Butler said. 'Wine can be cheaper than water here. The cheapest bottle of wine in the supermarket costs around 35p, and you can pay 55p for a plastic bottle of water.'

Brighton is a health-conscious place today, but even our fair city was being a bit balmy back in the 1980s when it attempted to try to get publicans – a profession known for their heavy drinking – to curtail their drinking habits. In 1986,

The Argus reported that the local authority had decided to limit the licensing hours of a conference for more than 1,000 publicans. The convention for the LVNH (the Licensed Victuallers' National Homes) traditionally partied on after their conferences ended late in the night – going on until 4 a.m sometimes. However, the organisers for the 1986 Brighton event at the Metropole and Brighton Centre were shocked to find out local magistrates would only grant them extra time until 12 midnight on Sunday and 2 a.m. on Friday and Saturday. The LVNH argued that the shortened hours would cost thousands of pounds, prevent their bands playing (who were booked for 2 a.m.) and cost Brighton a lot of good will. As press officer Ted Elkins explained, 'Pub landlords are known to be late-night revellers – they finish work at 11 and then want to unwind.'

Sussex as a whole must be a healthy place as, despite the determination of publicans to drink lots, as we have seen above, and the smoky atmospheres that existed before the smoking ban, we seem to have had some exceedingly old innkeepers. George and Mary Haflette seem to win top prize as they ran the Ram, east of Brighton in Firle, East Sussex, for seventy-seven years. When George and Mary finally gave up the licence in 1985 they still had a till that was able to give change from a sovereign. Brighton comes in a worthy second place, though, with George and Jessie Thomas, who ran The Eastern in Eastern Road Brighton for twenty-one years and celebrated their golden wedding anniversary in 1987. Their brewers Whitbread threw a surprise party for them at the Madeira Hotel, even bringing down a coachload of their friends from London for them. Jessie (seventy) and George (seventy-four) enjoyed a great night only eighteen months before the pub was closed for demolition due to Eastern Road being targeted for road

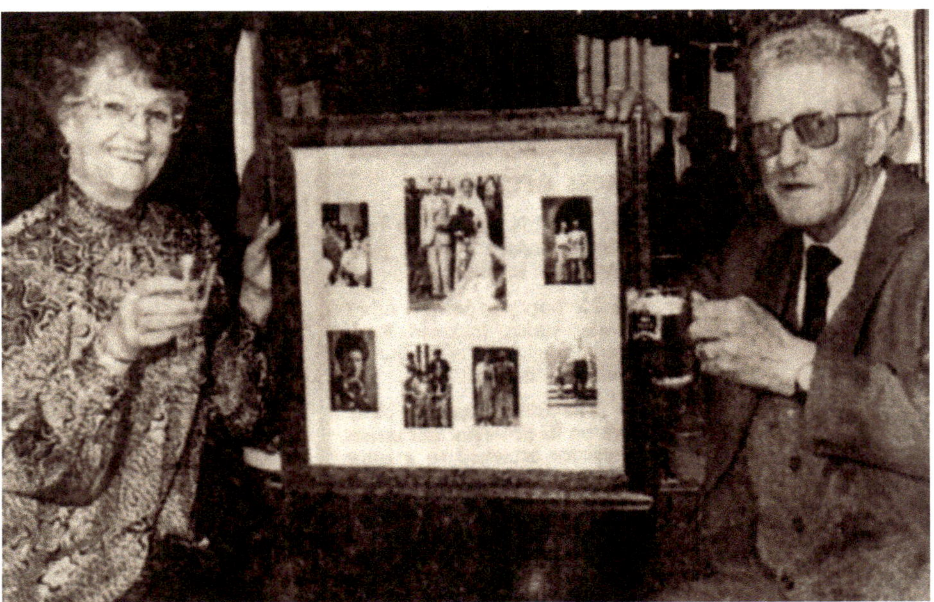

George and Jessie Thomas. (*The Argus*)

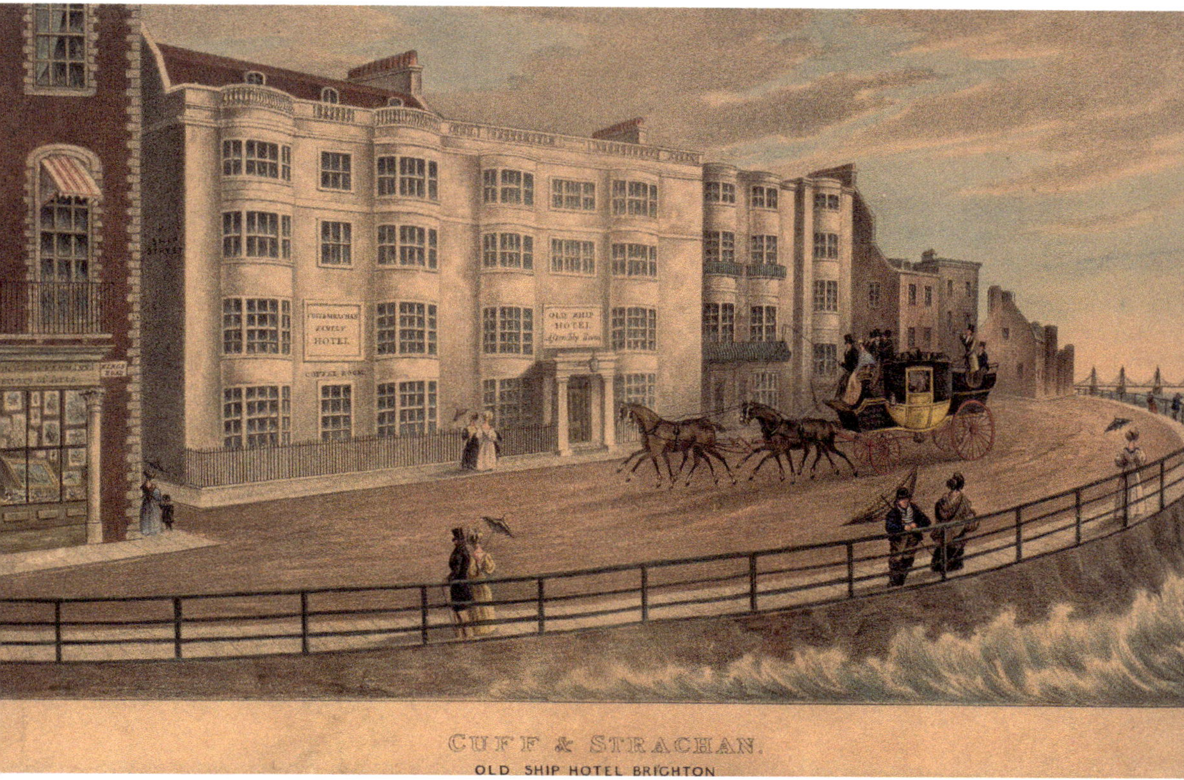

Old Ship Hotel.

widening. Jessie started off her career in French polishing before helping build Mosquito bombers in the Second World War; George served in both the Royal and Merchant Navy, seeing action in North Africa and Madagascar. The publican pair moved to Brighton after bringing their sons on holiday to Brighton's long-lost Black Rock campsite.

Health is linked to wealth and one way to slightly increase your wealth involving Brighton and Hove's hotels is, of course, to take home the complimentary goodies in your hotel room. Another, more illegal, way is stealing from hotels, which seemed to undergo a spike in the 1980s. Back in 1987 *The Argus* featured incredible (and sometime audacious) thefts from Brighton and Hove's many hotels, such as the guest at the Old Ship Hotel who decided to swipe a telephone from the desk of the hotel's reception. Being the 1980s, this was a relatively large landline handset connected to the desk, but this still didn't deter the persistent pilferer. In the article the hotel listed all of the thing you might imagine would have been stolen, such as ashtrays, teaspoons and towels, but incredibly the hotel's guests seemed to have a taste for stealing bath plugs. At the other end of the scale, the most ambitious theft seems to have been a large television set, which led to the staff chasing the thief down the road. A theft of a piano from the hotel's ballroom was thankfully thwarted – presumably by the room being upstairs in the Old Ship.

In those heavy-smoking days, Hove's Courtland Hotel was having to replace an incredible 250 personalised ashtrays every six months, costing 70p each. These thefts were somewhat less ambitious than the most successful hotel theft at this time, outside of Brighton at the Gatwick Hilton: a 6-foot-high tree in a huge earthenware pot was stolen out of the hotel lobby.

Another (illegal) way to remain wealthy is to check out of your Brighton hotel without paying your bill. As mentioned the most famous Brighton visitor to do this is Oscar Wilde, who left the Metropole in 1894 without paying (presumably due to his dire financial straits at the time). In 1992 the Chancellor of the Exchequer at that time, Norman Lamont, was thought to have done the same. The Conservative minister appeared to have checked out without paying his £900 bill after a four-day stay. The national press had a field day about it, but it turned out that an administrative backlog at the five-star hotel had led to a delay in it sending out accounts. One slightly later visitor definitely didn't settle his bill at the Grand though. In December 1996, a Danish visitor to the town claimed he was writing his thesis on public attitudes and wanted to find out how he was treated when under suspicion, so he ran up unpaid bills. The courts took less kindly to his 'experiment' and bailed him to a hostel. He then fled from Brighton to Denmark – presumably without paying his bill there either.

To keep mentally healthy, many Brightonians enjoy interactions with all creatures great and small and the amazing Sea Life Centre is always a good place for this. It wouldn't have been recommended though to interact with one past tankful of its creatures when back in 2006 it housed sea snakes. The Sea Life Centre became the first aquarium in the UK to house these special serpents, each with enough poison to kill three people – and that was just in one bite! Thankfully an antidote was on hand, though it had to be sent all the way from the same place as the snakes – Australia. No Brightonians ever touched the serpents, but one of our politicians tried to engage with scary sea (or, at least, loch) creatures four decades earlier. Kemp Town's MP in the 1960s, David James, had the honour of setting up the Bureau for the Investigation of the Loch Ness Monster.

Brighton was the location that a unique businesswoman set up a health and beauty business that has had an impact worldwide. Anita Roddick started off The Body Shop in Kensington Gardens and from day one it wasn't just about selling goods, it was about doing good, with an ethical outlook that set the stage for today's social enterprises, fair trade insistence and belief in sustainability. With stores around the world today, The Body Shop showed the world how to trade fairly and kindly and the late, great Anita set high streets alight from the 1970s with an eco-friendly business ethic that summed up the place of its birth well. Anita also took the shop's name from a local panel-beating car garage, who subsequently took umbrage with her choice. Anita, being a shrewd businesswoman, used their legal challenge to gain extra publicity for her fledgling business. The green colour the shops used was because Anita first used that colour green to cover up the mould growing in the Kensington Gardens shop! The most inspired touch from

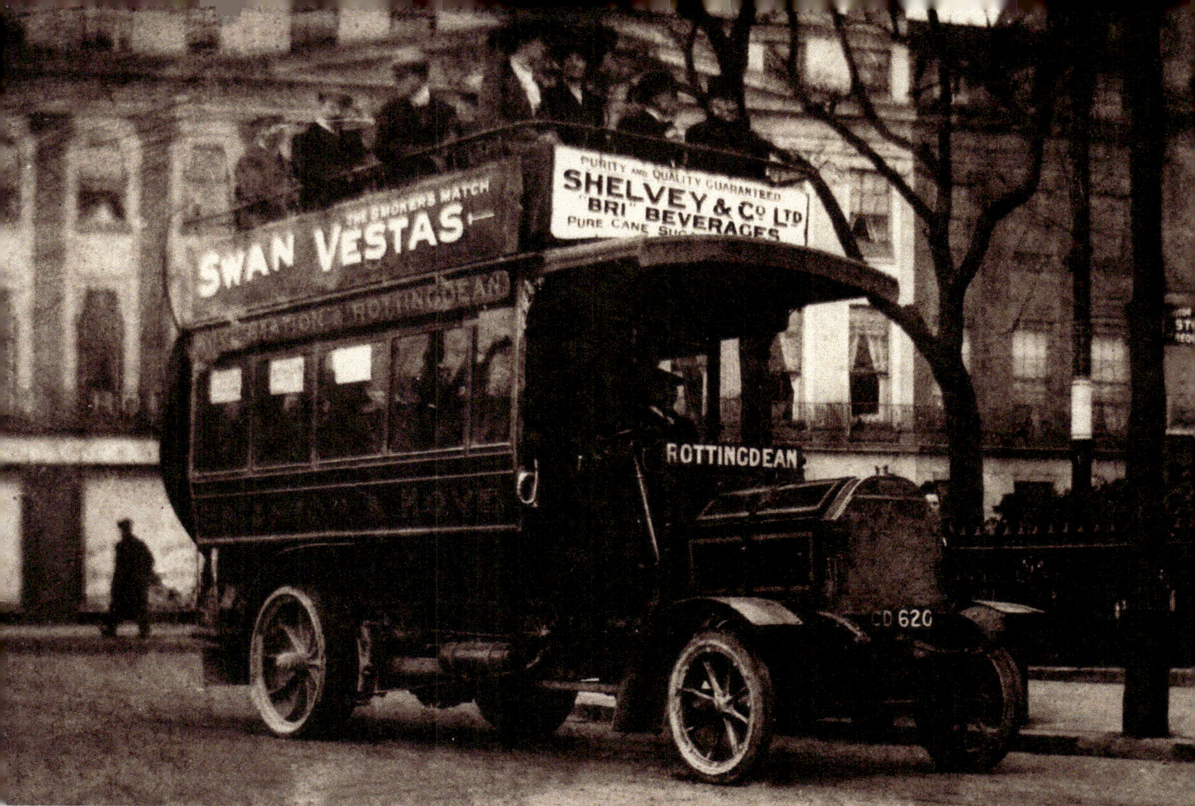

An early Brighton Bus.

the early days of The Body Shop was that Anita used urine-sample bottles to contain her first creams, lotions and body baths.

Brighton and Hove's buses are also to be celebrated for being another eco-friendly successful local business, as befitting the only city in the UK with a Green MP. Brighton and Hove Buses were one of the first in the industry to use low-sulphur fuel as soon as it became available, and it is also a market leader in the fitting of specialist equipment to reduce pollution of exhaust gases from bus engines. They have also been increasing the use of hybrid and biodiesel-using engines. Brighton has always led the way with eco-friendly transport, though. Not only did we have the world's first continually running passenger electric railway, leading the way in non-polluting transport from the 1880s, but we also held exhibitions a century later on the environment, years before being environmentally friendly was fashionable. The Metropole's Scitech exhibition in 1989 had local schools and universities all demonstrating how they were keeping green and highlighted the dangers of polluting rivers and of lead in the atmosphere.

Brighton ambulance men and women are definitely local heroes who promote health. For 365 days a year they zip around Brighton and Hove's streets, no matter how hilly or badly parked the cars they have to get past. Brighton has a pioneering history of past paramedic achievement and inventing equipment that not many people know about. Brightonian Douglas Chamberlain not only invented the first defibrillator, saving countless lives, but is also responsible for the establishment of the first paramedic organisation in Britain.

Ideas, Inventions and Inventors

Brighton and Hove today is a hugely inventive and creative city, which follows on from historical trends of it being a birthplace of new and innovative ideas and inventions. From Bucky Balls to the Daddy Long Legs, from the 1360 to early electric-powered buses, cars and Volk's Railway, Brighton has seen new and novel ideas and inventions start here or has played a part in their development.

There has been much speculation over the years as to where Brighton gained its name and who 'invented' or gave us the name. Brighton itself has had a number

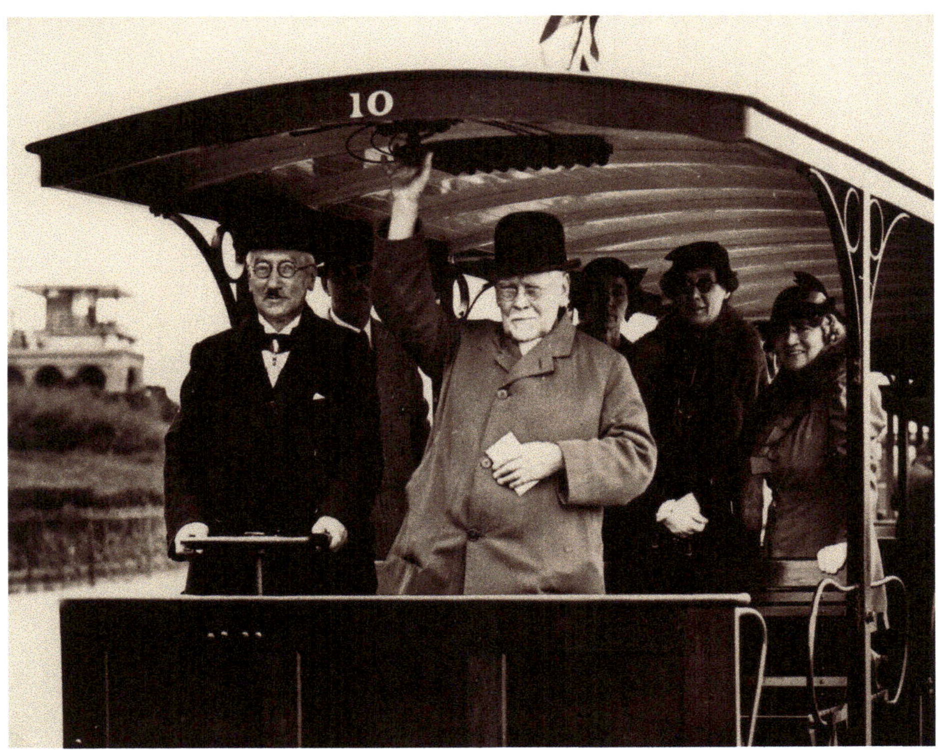

Above and opposite: Volk's Electric Railway.

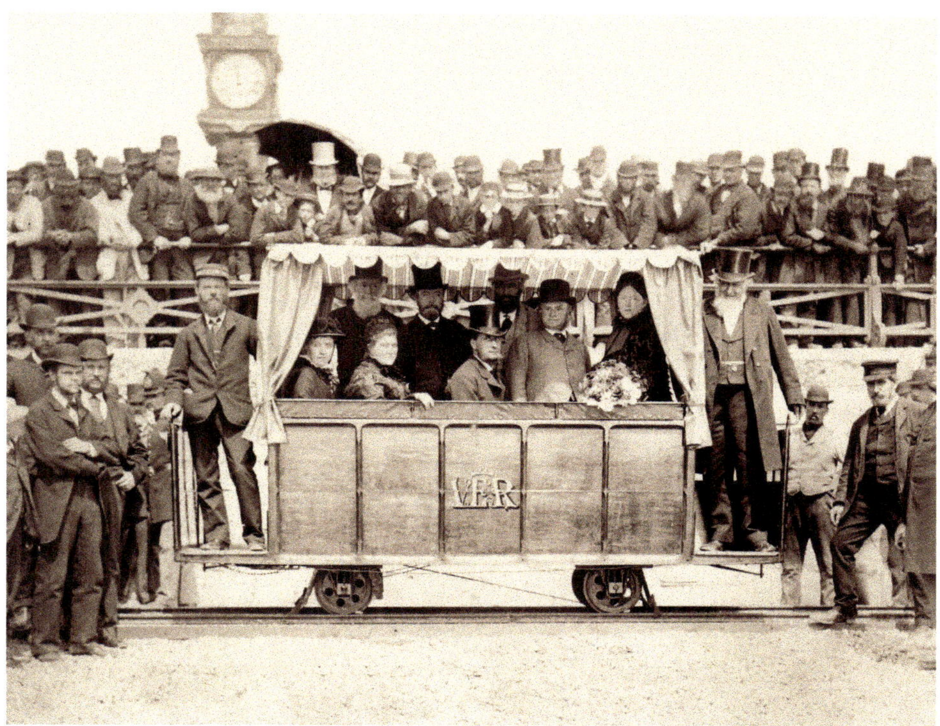

of names over the years, with its current title first appearing only in the 1660s and being adopted officially in 1810. Before that we were the wordy Brighthelmston(e), which itself evolved over time from Bristelmestune and Beorthelmstone. The name would suggest a Saxon leader or man of importance called Beorthelm established a 'tun' or 'homestead' early on in Anglo-Saxon times. Interestingly, the name is similar to that of an early Archbishop of Canterbury, Byrhthelm or Beorthelm, who died in AD 973. He was the Bishop of Wells in 956 before briefly becoming Archbishop of Canterbury in 959. He started life as a monk from Glastonbury Abbey and was not far from the town as he was involved in restoring lands around the Selsey area to the church. These had been seized by a man named Ælfsige, thought to have been the Bishop of Winchester. This would mean Brighton has religious beginnings.

Only in Brighton could you get inspiration for invading aliens, a rollercoaster for royalty and an aid to the German war effort all in the same package. And that package was the 'Daddy Long Legs', or if you want its official title, the BARSET (Brighton and Rottingdean Seashore Electric Railway). The machine itself had the name of *Pioneer*, which it certainly was. Years ahead of its time, it was a moving tramway on legs and ran along a set of rails on concrete blocks, some of which can be still seen today at low tide. It looked like a section of the Palace Pier had broken away and was rebelling! Amazingly, the motor that powered this railway through water was powered by electricity. Not a common mix, but unbelievably it worked for four years without electrocuting anyone. Its 2–4 mph ride was experienced by

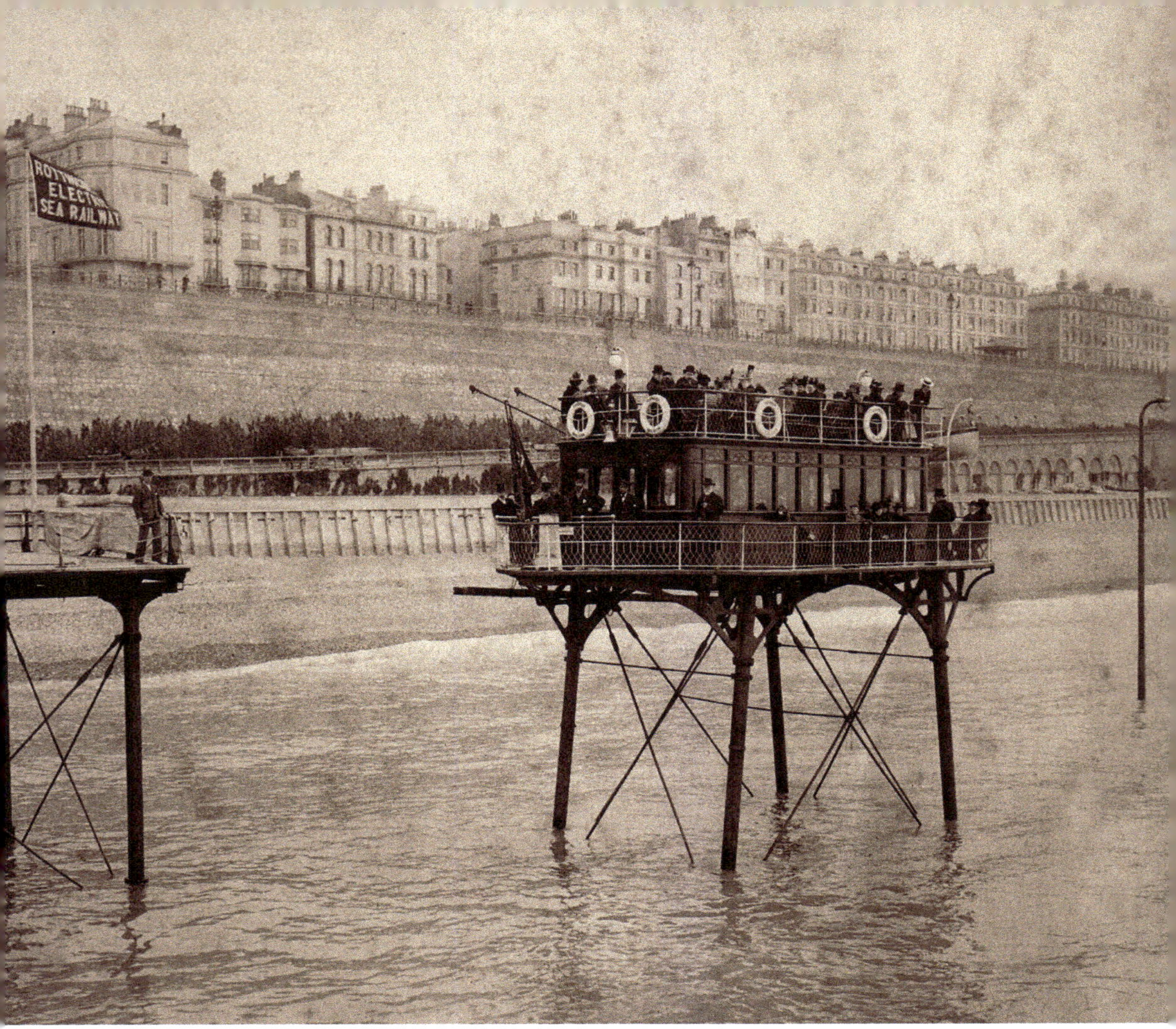

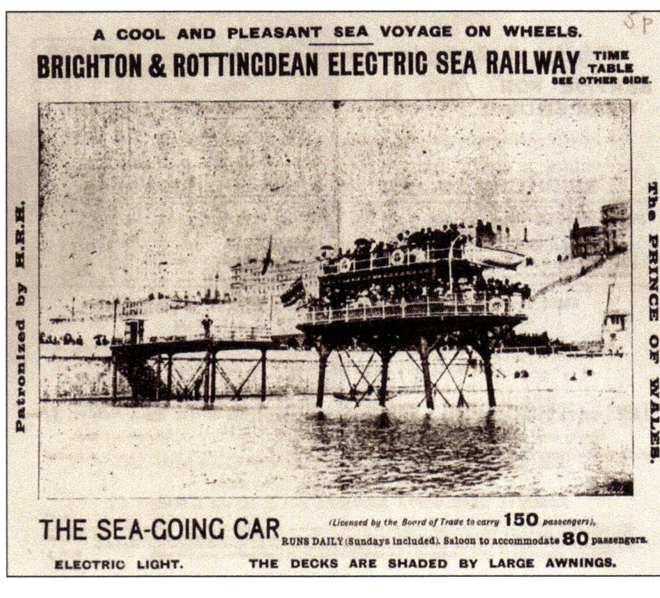

Above and left: Volk's Electric Railway Mk II: 'The Daddy Long Legs'.

royals, VIPs and the well-to-do from across the world, and is even said to have inspired H.G. Wells' design for the invading aliens in *The War of the Worlds*.

Fortunately nobody was hurt when *Pioneer* was blown over in the terrible storms at the end of the nineteenth century, but it may well have ended its days hurting British people in a different way. The *Pioneer* stopped working only a few years after it started due to Brighton Council demanding its creator reroute the track around newly needed sea defences and their failing to insure it for storm damage. It remained moored to the pier at Ovingdean, which passengers had used to embark on westwards journeys until 1910, rusting away until it was eventually sold for scrap to Germany. The metal, it is thought, would have ended up as part of the German war machine in the First World War.

Magnus Volk, designer of the Daddy Long Legs, was our greatest ever inventor. His life was one of hard work, creativity and inventiveness – the *Pioneer* being just one of his inventions. Like the Cohen family, who did so much for Brighton, his family also came from Germany and his father was a clockmaker. He was responsible for lighting the Pavilion, Brighton's first telephone call and exchange,

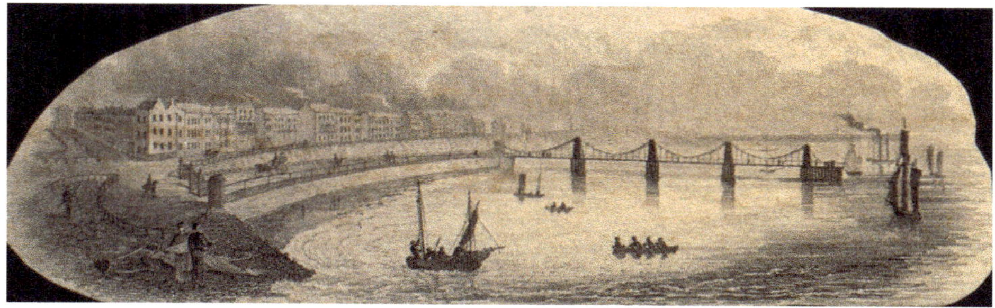

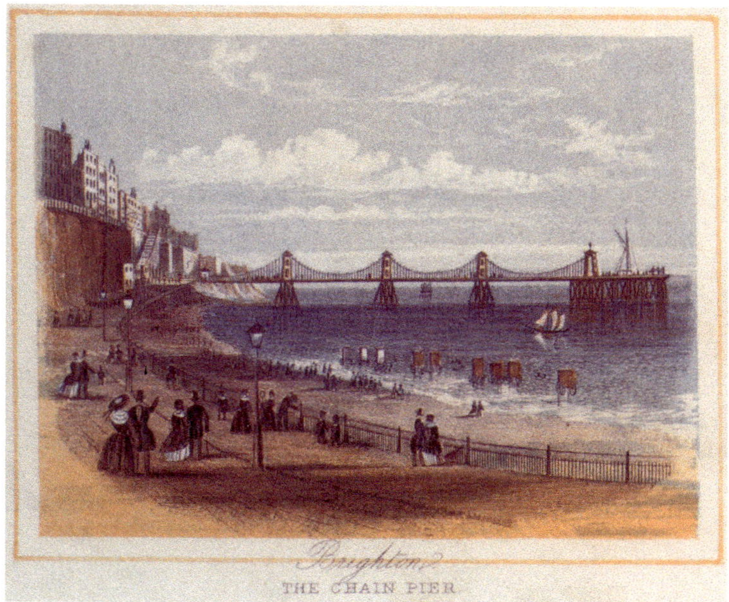

Above and right:
The Chain Pier.

bringing seaplanes to Brighton and, most importantly, an even older railway than the *Pioneer*: Britain's first electric passenger railway and the oldest existing electric railway in the world, known as Volk's Railway. While doing all this he also managed to oversee other projects around the country. Back in Brighton, his first workshop in Preston Street produced some of the first electric apparatus in the country and his house in Preston Road was Brighton's first to have electric light. By 1883 he had been entrusted to introduce electricity into the Pavilion. That same year, on 4 August, he opened his first electric railway, which ran from the aquarium to the Chain Pier. It was a huge success, and 20,000 passengers were carried in the first year. The following year the track was extended to opposite Paston Place, and by 1900 to Black Rock. Despite the collapsed Chain Pier colliding with it, ongoing storm damage (the early years of the railway saw it run high above the beach as the sea came in much further a century ago) and vandalism from jealous cabbies, it survived and continued to grow in popularity. By 1900, the Daddy Long Legs was also running alongside his first railway. Volk then went on to build an electric car and X-ray equipment, and the success with his beachside railway led to confidence in introducing trams across Brighton and inspired the electrification of the Southern Railway network in 1933. He even attempted an electric bus service from the beach going up Wilson Avenue to the Downs. By 1926 the ten cars in his railway's fleet were carrying a staggering 1 million passengers a year. Despite plans to close the railway and move it to a park or replace it with a monorail over the years, Brighton's historic railway is still going strong and in its fifteenth decade. Volk's first environmentally friendly form of transport serves to not only remind us of this Brighton genius, but also that Brighton was at the forefront of green developments over a century ago.

Volk was also involved with the town's central clock, ensuring that the Jubilee Clock Tower at the top of Brighton's West Street was graced with a spherical copper time ball, which would rise up a pole and drop on the hour at 1 p.m. as a visual timing signal (similar to the time ball at Greenwich Observatory). The idea was that, like Greenwich, it could be used by passing shipping to synchronise their clocks. The ball's hydraulic operation was disabled in 1902 after numerous complaints from locals about the loud whistling noise that it made, which apparently startled horses and annoyed shopkeepers. Despite this, the idea for public clocks really caught on and Brighton is today a city of clock towers due to our Victorian and Edwardian ancestors. The ball was restored a century after its disablement at a cost of £100,000. Many other clocks were built, but none had a celebratory perfume at their grand unveiling like the 'The Jubilee Clock Tower Bouquet'. The best reason for building one of the other clock towers must be that of the one for Queen's Park Clock Tower. The park was formally opened to the public on 10 August 1892 and it gained its clock tower twenty years later after a local tradesmen, William Godleye, left £1,000 in his will for a clock tower to be built. The reason for his generosity was because when visiting the park, he'd always been pestered by children asking him the time.

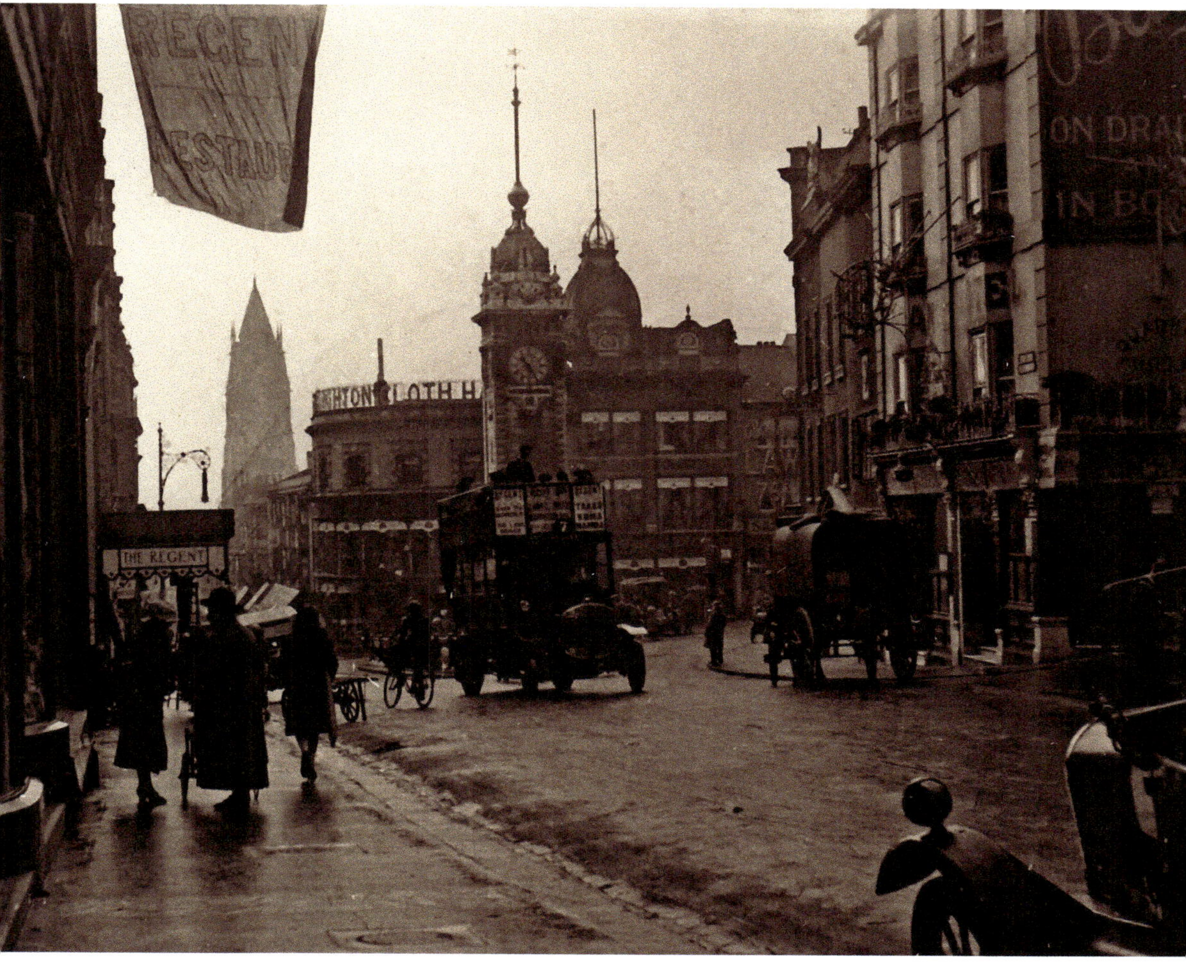

The Jubilee Clock Tower.

Brighton is a fashionable city, of course, but the most fantastic innovation for footwear appeared at Hove's County Cricket Ground. The County Ground horse pulled the roller between innings to flatten down the turf and was clad in his very own unique pair of bespoke leather booties. These ensured that the turf wasn't trounced by his hooves.

Brighton and Hove may love horses, but it has had a love-hate relationship with the car over time. The city has built cars, had a car museum for a while, hosted speed trials and is the end point of the Veteran Car Run – the annual race that begins in London. Today the city has turned away from the car and is trying to be as eco-friendly as possible, with Brighton bikes and one of the country's most successful bus companies. This might be a wise move when we look at some of the 'car-lamities' that have taken place in the county in the past. Firstly, a Sussex firm was once given the task of improving the look of one of the cars built by Reliant, the company that built the three-wheeled Reliant Robin, similar to the Rialto

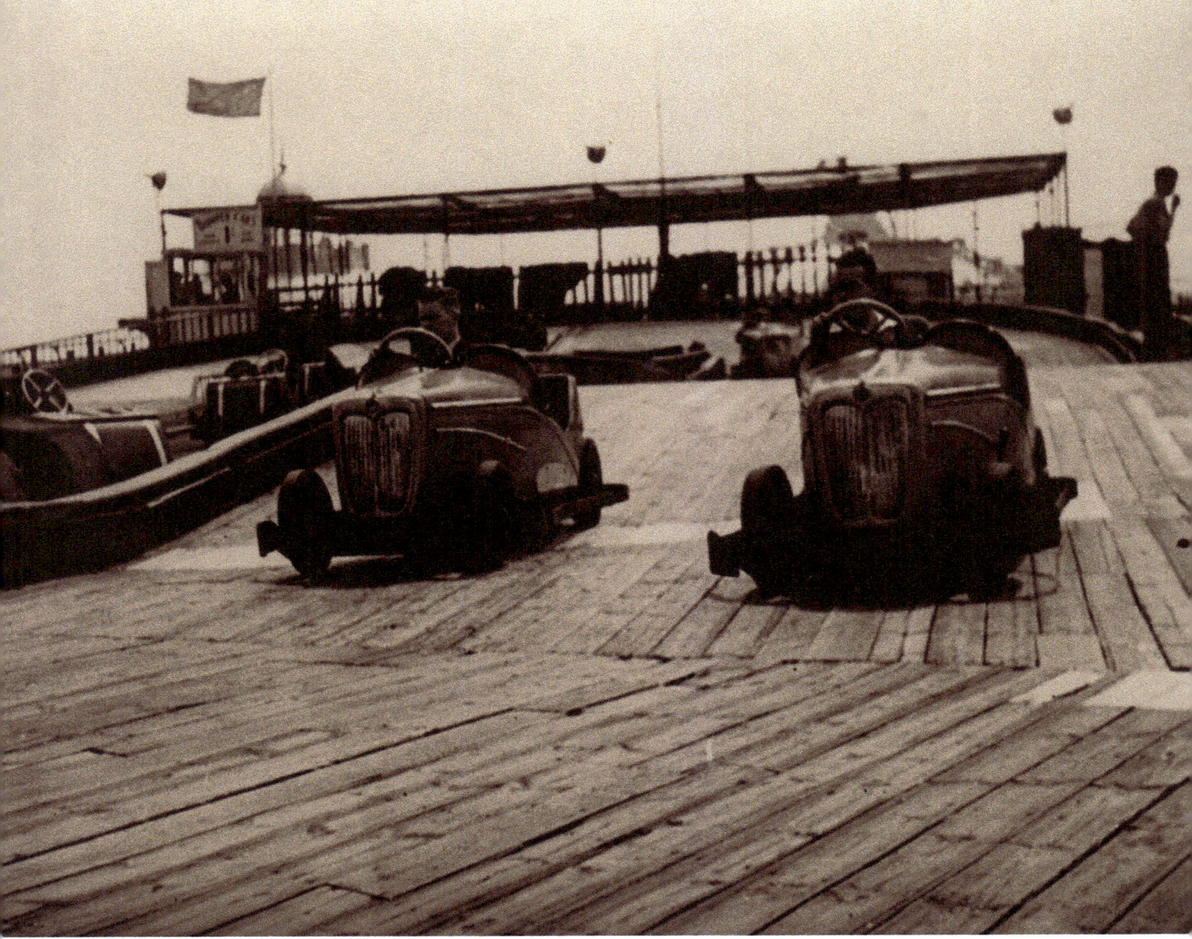

van so beloved by Del Boy in *Only Fools and Horses*. By the late 70s, Reliant was in trouble. With a recall of 25,000 Robins, an image crisis and recession. The car company dropped the 'Robin' name and was given a refreshed look by International Automotive Design of Sussex. The car became more angular than its predecessor, with a plastic grille on the front and headlights borrowed from the Austin Metro, but still failed to ensure the long-term future of the company. The Brighton Railway Works was the home for another automotive works – the Isetta factory from 1957 until 1964. Not only was the bubble car itself unique, but so was the car factory as it had no road access! Cars leaving the factory faced a downhill journey down a flight of 100 steps, so finished products destined for the road left via rail.

Brighton is an innovative place as we all know, but one pub landlord back in the early 1990s came up with a whole new concept: the pub that deliberately tries to make its customers as miserable as possible. And no, it's not Wetherspoons. *The Argus* reported back in 1992 about Brighton's grumpiest guvnor. This was Ian Thomas who was proud of the fact that his bar – Bianco's – had a hideous pink interior and he had a reputation for being miserable. He moaned about the fact that he had to be cleaner, barman and

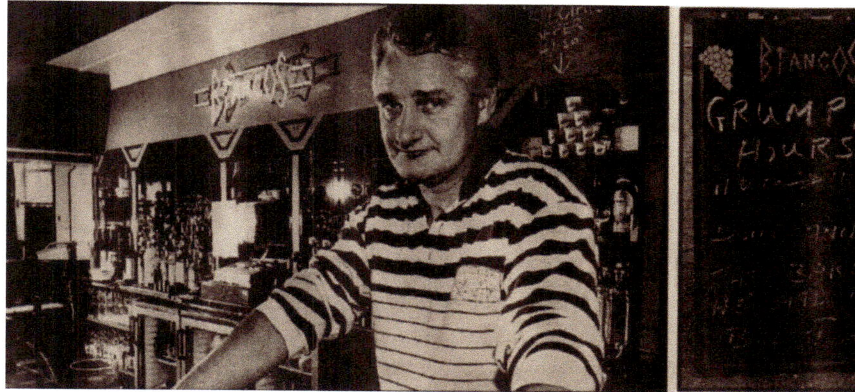

Ian Thomas. (*The Argus*)

doorman despite this was due to him laying off all seven staff just two days after taking over. Bizarrely, the pub's takings soared in the first ten days that Ian was in charge, despite his stock line of 'What the hell do you want?' when asked for a drink, hefty prices and moaning at customers to sit up straight. Fittingly for such a dour drinking hole, the pub had not a happy hour but a grumpy hour, repeated from 11 a.m. to 11 p.m.

Dark Star Brewery is much less grumpy and has been a huge success story, being sold off in February 2018 to London-based brewer Fuller Smith & Turner, and now Japanese brewers Asahi. Its biggest-selling brew, Hophead, is subsequently sold even more widely around the South, but it started off in a Brighton pub cellar with two innovative men. Our local paper, *The Argus*, featured the earliest days of the brewery back in January 1996 when it talked about Dark Star being a 'pint-sized brewery' and a 'microbrewery', 'squeezed into the tiny cellar' of the Evening Star pub in Surrey Street, Brighton. It also mentioned the brewery's founder, Rob Jones, who first brewed a beer called Dark Star in London before moving production to Brighton. The first batch of ales Jones brewed in the Brighton pub were tested by the Evening Star's regulars, and the landlord of the Star (Geoff Brown) hinted at the brewery's early promise as he was 'delighted with sales'. The article talked about the brewery's early beers, which included not one but four ginger beers, a winter beer called Winter Solstice (brewed with coriander), as well as the award-winning Dark Star beer. It told how Jones used his own recipes and how Geoff Brown correctly predicted 'some great plans for the next few months'. Little did they know a quarter of a century on just how popular the brewery's beers would be and how it would go from micro to massive-sales brewery, with a wealth of other Sussex microbrewers following its successes. So, let's celebrate Dark Star and all the other breweries with Brighton in their DNA who help us with our celebrations.

We finish this chapter with a celebration of Brighton's scientific excellence by talking balls. Buckyballs to be precise. Harry Kroto at Sussex University, along with his US collaborators, recently revealed that carbon can exist as tiny spherical

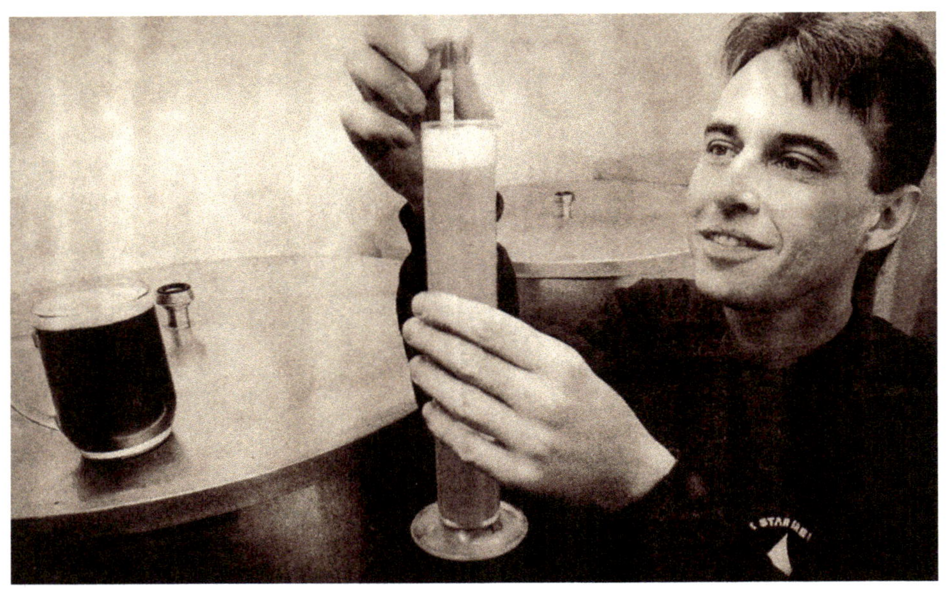

Rob Jones of Dark Star Brewery testing early ales. (*The Argus*)

molecules, now known as 'fullerenes' or 'buckyballs'. Our universities here in Sussex have world-class scientific facilities, and a matching reputation. Even other academics recognise the worth of Brighton's two universities. Sir Paul Nurse, chancellor of the University of Bristol, has said he chose the University of Sussex for his work earlier in his career as it had a strong tradition in bacterial molecular genetics and an excellent reputation in biology.

The Dark Star Brewery today, now relocated to Partridge Green.

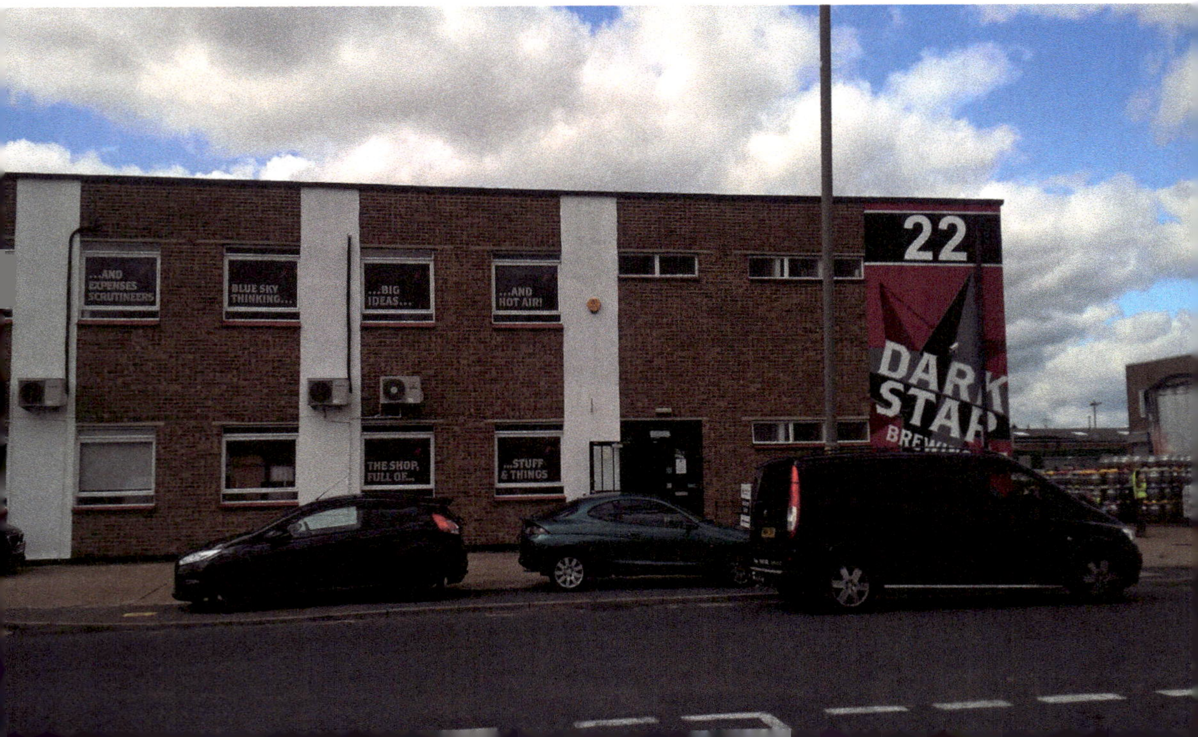

Local Heroes

Any celebration of Brighton and Hove must remember those men and women who fought to save the town from invasion and attack. Numerous books have been dedicated to this subject though, and so we can only give a brief flavour of this here and turn instead to more unusual heroes: those who have entertained us, made a difference or just made Brighton and Hove a better place to live.

Brighton has always been known for its green credentials – it has the country's first Green Party MP – but one man took this to extremes back in the early 1800s. A man by the name of Cope was referred to simply as 'The Green Man' and seemed to have been known by, well, nobody, but witnessed by everyone at the time. He dressed in green pantaloons, a waistcoat, frock coat and cravat, which all reflected to make him look green all over. Years before vegetarianism (nobles in the Middle Ages thought veg made you ill), he ate nothing but greens, fruits and vegetables. Even his habitat was green: he furnished his rooms green, had a green sofa, green chairs, tables, bed and curtains. Even when out and about his gig, portmanteau, gloves, livery and whip were all green. It didn't stop there, though, he had a green silk handkerchief and large watch chain with green seals that was fastened to his waistcoat's green buttons. If only he had met Diane Moran, the 'Green Goddess' of 1980s *BBC Breakfast*.

Our next heroes are both councillors. The first can justly be called the man who saved the Royal Pavilion from destruction. Lewis Sleight is not a Brighton name most people know, but we should. In the 1840s, Queen Victoria decided to sell the Pavilion as she found it too small and felt the people of the town intruded on her privacy. Buildings sprouting up across the town also meant that the building no longer had the sea view the Prince Regent had enjoyed from his bedroom. She transferred the furniture to Buckingham Palace and the land looked set to be sold for development. While waiting for the Corporation to vote on whether it should be purchased by the town at a cost of £53,000, Lewis Sleight went secretly to London and purchased it for the town anyway as the Forestry Commission (who owned the land) had decided to sell it. The debate over approving the purchase by the council rattled on for many years. Finally, in a vote won by a majority of just thirty-seven, the Pavilion was saved for Brighton. And at only at least a tenth of the cost the prince had paid to build it!

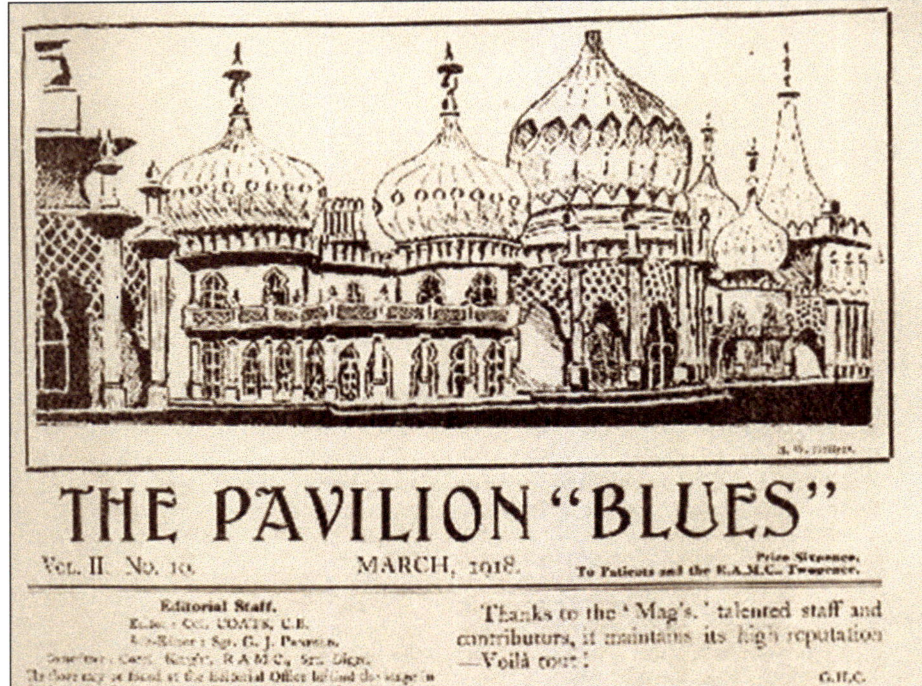

THE PAVILION "BLUES"

Vol. II. No. 10.   MARCH, 1918.   Price Sixpence.
To Patients and the R.A.M.C. Twopence.

Editorial Staff.
Editor: Col. COATS, C.B.
Sub-Editor: Sgt. G. J. Pearce.
Secretary: Capt. Knight, R.A.M.C., Sec. Dip.
The Committee may be found at the Editorial Office behind the stage in the Recreation Room, and are always open to receive suggestions for the improvement of this Mag.

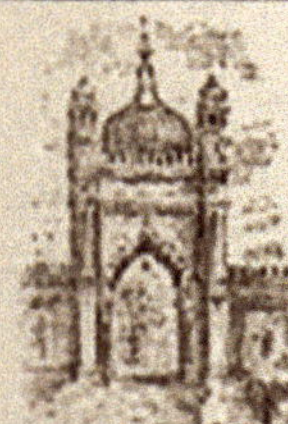

Editor's Foreword.
The 'Mag.' joins hands in according a hearty welcome to Colonel G. T. K. Maurice, c.m.g., a.m.s., on his succeeding to the command of the P.G.H.

The Editor has been in extremis to find blocks to build up this forward and trembled to launch it in its nettless condition.

His qualms have been calmed by the wily 'Sub,' who, in his Sub-Editorial, with his usual knack of expressing himself 'elegantly,' has pronounced the effort a fluent article! Bravo it, 'Sub'—the rejuvenating effect of eight days 'excused duty' has made you write with elegance!) The boot is on the 'Sub's' leg—the Editor cannot put his into such a brilliant covering.

Thanks to the 'Mag's.' talented staff and contributors, it maintains its high reputation —Voilà tout!

G.H.C.

___

A Sub-Editorial.
Another month has elapsed and again I find it my painful duty to inflict upon you another monstrosity.

Since the last issue of this journal I have been 'excused duty' for eight days. After obtaining the necessary permission, passes and warrants, I hied me to the city known as 'The Smoke,' there to spend a brief period of time with my people. What a comfortable feeling it is to be at home! The cheerful fireside, the group of friends, the homely cooking (when there is food to cook—No! I did not starve, far from it), and the unlimited freedom. It is said that one does not appreciate anything to the full until they have lost it. I do love my home since I have been away from it. Time went all too quickly —I could have filled another ten days with the greatest of ease, but here I am —back in the old spot, 'in harness.' My sojourn in the 'smoke' was not without excitement. 'Fritz'

Magazine produced by patients at the Pavilion hospital for limbless men, 1916-1920.

Weighing around 20 tons, the Goldstone in Hove Park is a remnant of sandstone and flint that was left after the erosion of the much softer terrain around it. Legend has it as being a clump of the Downs kicked by the Devil as he tried to break through the hills by digging a route for the sea to flood the pious and godly people of the Weald. It took its name either from 'godstone' or 'goldstone', either of which suggests

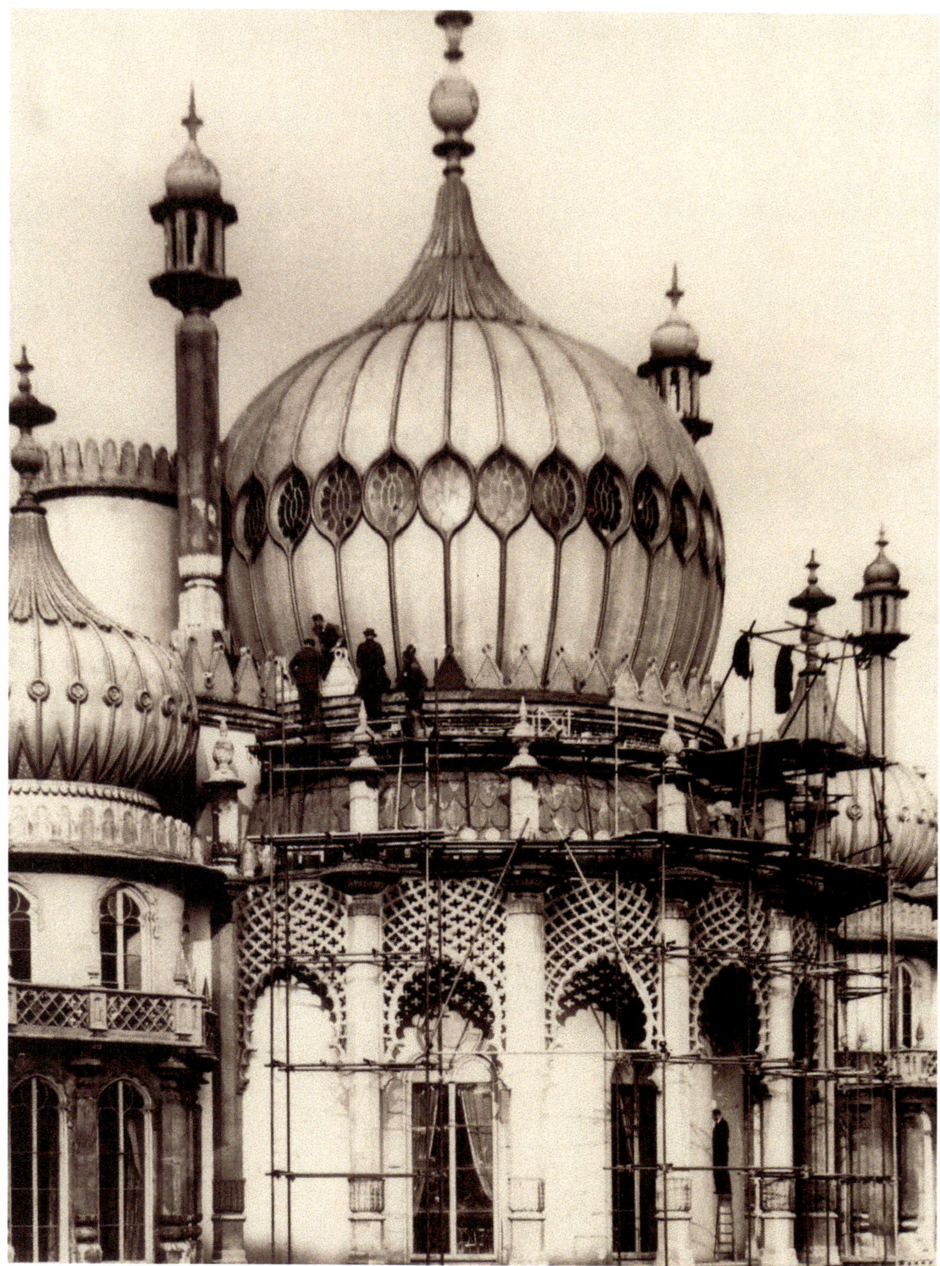

it had some holy purpose in the past. It was likely to have been worshipped due to flint and sandstone being unusual for the area in its original location. There are mentions in some records of it seeming to have a face appearing naturally on one of its sides. Its supposed use by druids led to it being known as the 'Druid's Altar'. By 1834 its original home (east of Sackville Road) had changed from a remote lawless area to a popular tourist spot. So popular, in fact, that in that year the farmer who owned Goldstone Bottom had it buried, where it remained until 1900 when it was brought to the new Hove Park by Councillor William Hollamby who first located and excavated the rock. It became a major feature of the new park and the newly created Brighton and Hove Albion's first proper ground took its name from the farm the rock gave its name to. Brighton and Hove Albion's Goldstone Ground was demolished in 1997 and the rock today, which is across from the ground's former location, reminds us of this much-loved sporting site. It should also remind us of the foresight of local hero Councillor Hollamby, without whom our biggest football club's first stadium might have had a different name and the club's history would be very different.

Arthur Wagner, vicar of Brighton back in Victorian times, dedicated much of his time to helping 'fallen women'. Queens Square (where the taxi rank is, opposite Churchill Square) once had a number of buildings for housing women trying to take Sting's advice and realise they didn't have to 'put on the red light'. Brighton had a reputation for ladies of the oldest profession in Victorian times, with both Valley Gardens and New Street by the Theatre Royal being remarked upon for the large numbers of ladies offering their services. Moving into the twentieth century, however, Brighton gained a vicar who presumably wouldn't have batted an eyelid at any vice the city had to offer. Canon John Hester took over the role Wagner had been in a century earlier, and his earlier parish made Brighton look like Hay-on-Wye. Before moving to Brighton in 1975, he had previously been rector of Soho and his parish contained numerous adult shops, fifty strip clubs and numerous adult cinemas.

The Goldstone, Hove Park.

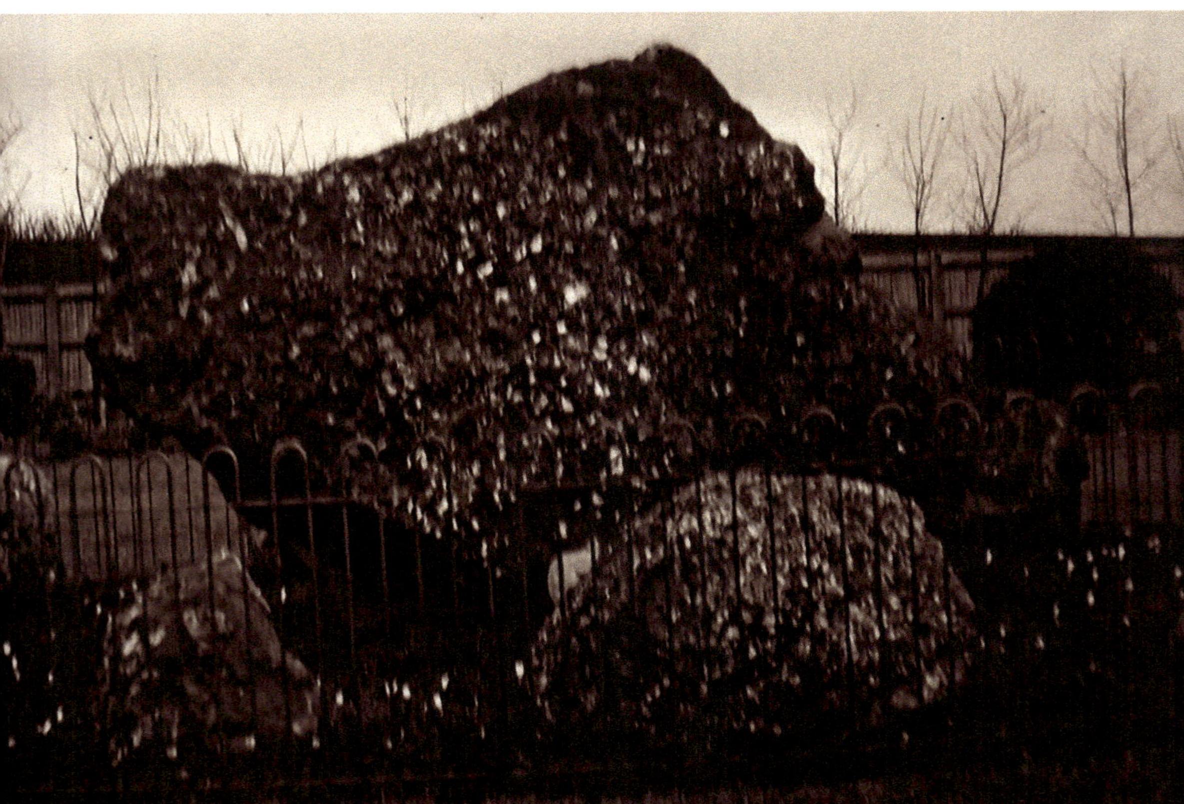

Brighton has a history of film, photos and filming, with numerous films made in the town and early photography shops from the 1840s. The town's first photographic studio was in Marine Parade and opened in 1841. Its opening day was graced by none other by the world-renowned painter William Constable, who famously painted Brighton's Chain Pier. Brighton even had one of the country's first female photographers: Agnes Ruge, who had a daguerreotype business based in Western Road. Communism caused her to meet her husband, who had fled the Continent with Karl Marx. They were associates and so he was in the UK in exile due to his political beliefs. Brighton is incredibly photogenic so it is not surprising so many films have been set here, but the urge to record how Brighton looks is nothing new. Before the days of photography, there were more Victorian engravings made of Brighton & Hove than of any other town or city in the UK outside London.

The year 1857 was the one that Brighton's premiere architect, Amon Henry Wilds, died and was buried in Shoreham. Probably much reduced in wealth and long out of fashion, his final resting place was even widely forgotten for many years. All of which seems criminal when you realise that not only was he part of a triumvirate that designed much of what we think of when we think of Brighton and Hove today (such as Kemp Town, Brunswick Town and Regency Square), but he alone is responsible for even more. Amon Henry Wilds (1790–1857) was the son of Amon Wilds (1762–1833) who starting off in Lewes, moved to Brighton and, with Charles A. Busby, laid out many of the exclusive housing developments such as Kemp Town, which brought the wealthy and aristocracy to the sea. Wilds Jr was responsible for the Victoria Fountain in the Steine, Oriental Place, Park Crescent, Western Terrace and Montpelier Crescent, as well as the western extension and tombs in St Nicholas's Churchyard. He even provided the one intact architectural gem in the wasteland that is London Road as it approaches Preston

Regency Square.

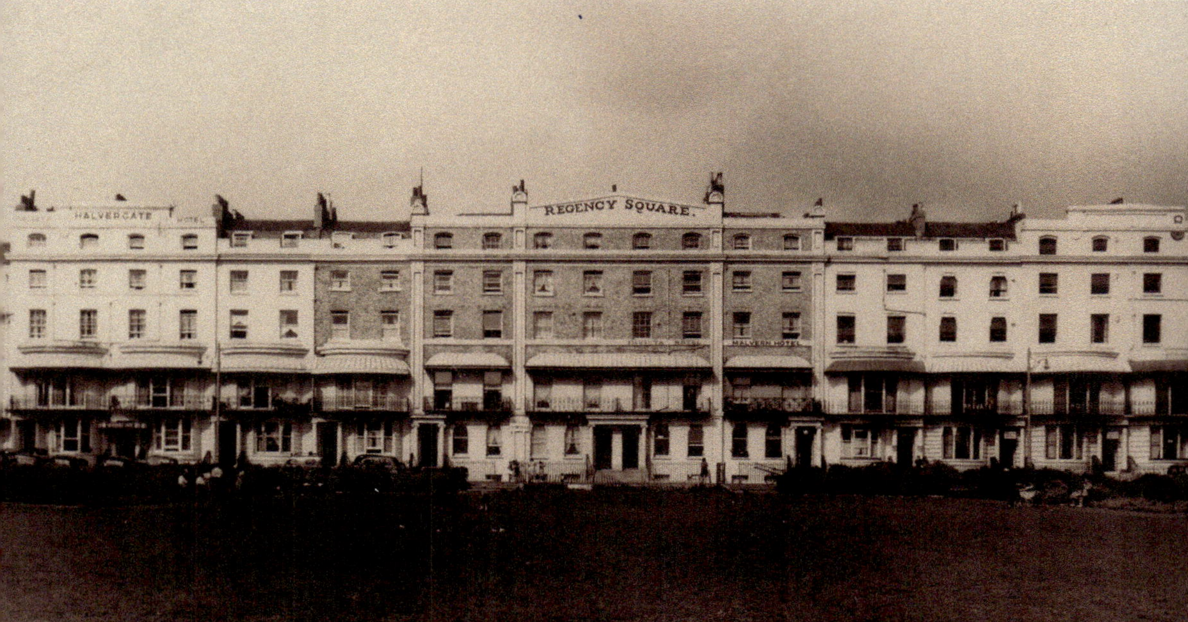

Circus – No. 87 London Road. Finally, he is responsible for not only laying out the trees that make up the Level but also for putting the elms into Elm Grove. It is hard not to like the man who built a mini-replica of the Royal Pavilion for himself to live in – the Western Pavilion off Western Road. But by the 1850s his star had waned and he was living in a small cottage overlooking the Adur by the new railway line at Shoreham. Sadly, the man who was able to provide one of Brighton's grandest graves – for his father Amon Wilds at St Nicholas's Church, decorated with his trademark ammonite shell design – wouldn't have the same done for him. His plain, miniscule grave was for many years even covered over with undergrowth, a less than fitting memorial for the man who did so much for the city's environment.

Brighton's landlords and landladies are definitely our heroes, keeping us topped up with our favourite tipples and helping us whet our whistles. The most unusual one, though, must be Albert of the (now demolished) Stag Inn in Upper Bedford Street, Kemp Town. What makes him unusual is not his love of beer (proved by once drinking a whole barrel of real ale) or the fact he dumped bottles of mineral water in a freezer making them explode, or tapping staff on the shoulder in the beer cellar. It's the fact that Albert died a century before he did all of these things, according to *The Argus* in February 1991. Despite Albert's goings-on, Taff Hills, landlord of the Stag at that time decreed that he was refusing to be scared, claiming 'I shall never be frightened off by the ghost!' despite not being able to sleep at night from Albert's antics. Albert was believed to be a previous landlord of the Stag who had hanged himself in the cellar and seemed to be making life as difficult as possible for his twentieth-century successors. Hill told *The Argus* he was ready to get a priest in to exorcise the 300-year-old pub, but Albert's activities perhaps had an effect as the pub was struggling by the 2000s and was demolished by 2013.

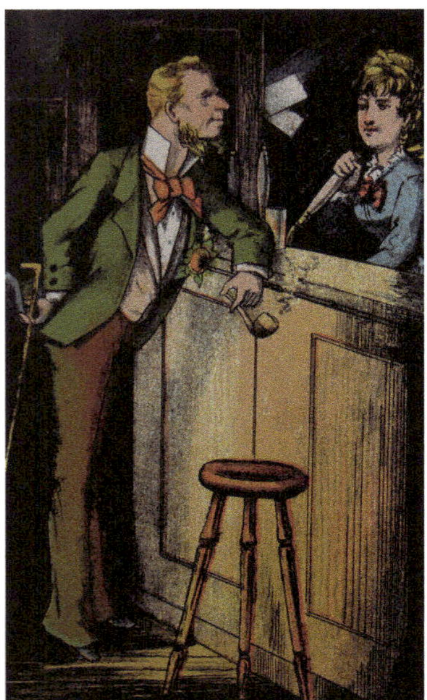

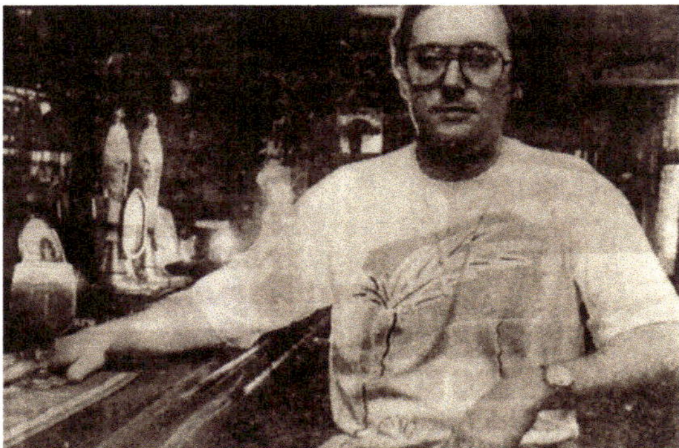

Above: Taff Hills, the spooked landlord of the Stag Inn. (*The Argus*)

Left: A valued landlady.

Things in Brighton move around without the help of the supernatural. When Brighton Aquarium's original entrance was due to be demolished in the 1920s, the town's Superintendent of parks, Captain Bertie MacLaren, removed the four figures of the seasons that adorned the clock tower above the entrance. They ended up in Preston Park's rose garden. The two great mythical beasts that had also welcomed aquarium guests were placed by the pool in front of the Rotunda in Preston Park and can still be seen there today, although two other rescued statues are now painted black and gold. MacLaren is also a great Brighton hero due to his amazing (but unfulfilled) plans for the aquarium. In 1924 it was thought the building should be modernised and so MacLaren offered a complete design for a building and gardens, believing it was 'the town's most important entrance to the sea'. He put forward a graceful open-air park and buildings that would be dominated by a raised platform. There was also to be a concert hall, which was to have a wagon-shaped roof of glass and (futuristically for the time) 'a prism glass floor electrically illuminated underneath' that couples would dance romantically upon. He also wanted the surrounding slopes laid out as a rock garden rather than being covered in concrete: 'In natural stratification … [offering] one blaze of colour all through the season.' MacLaren wasn't granted his wish as the plans were seen as unsuitable for a site bordering onto the sea, so we are thankfully left with our Victorian Sea Life Centre still today. Eugenius Birch, the aquarium's designer, would have an impact on the clock tower in Preston Park. Across the valley from this MacLaren was able to build his rock garden a decade later, using granite transported from Cheddar Gorge.

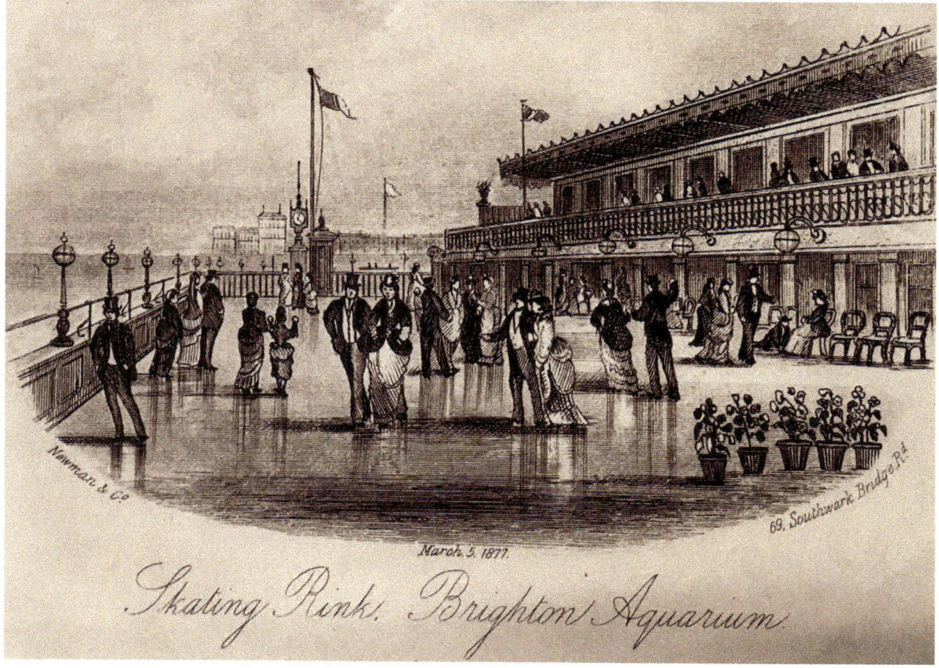

Skating rink at Brighton Aquarium – MacLaren had far grander plans than this for the site.

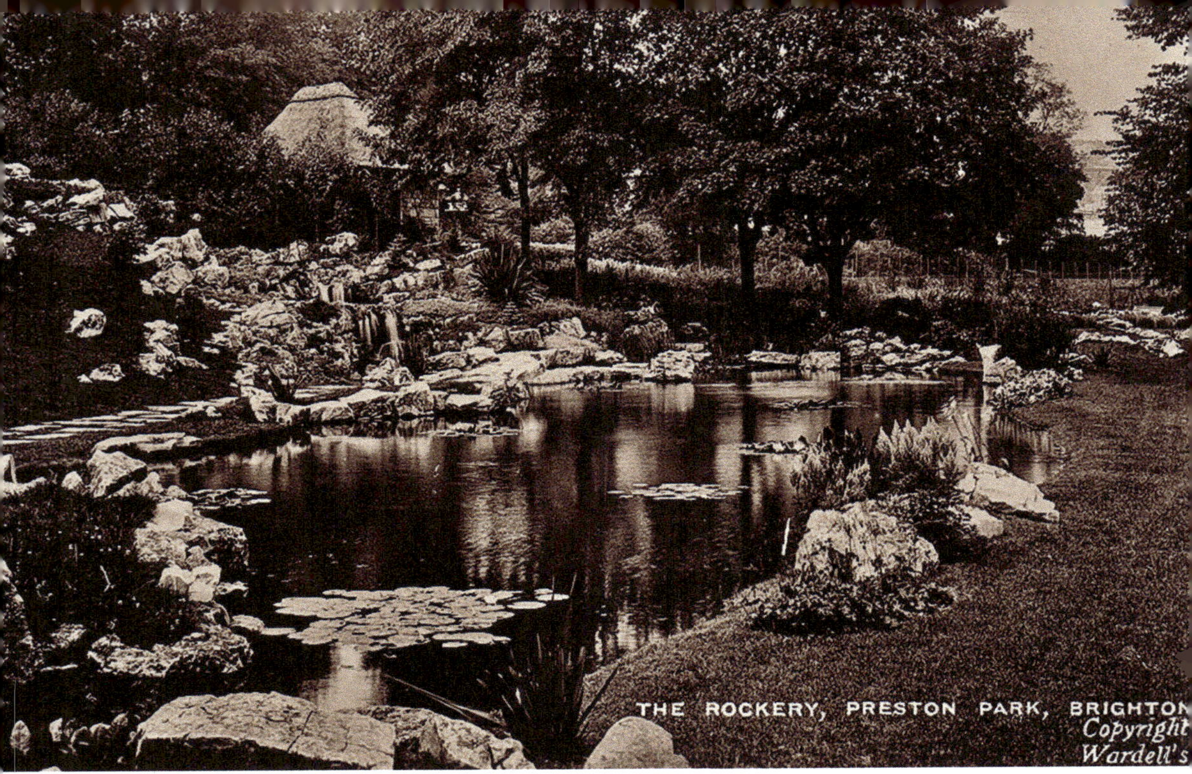

The Rockery.

MacLaren's plans didn't stop with the rockery, however. He also came up with a visionary scheme for the neighbouring 63-acre Preston Park that Brighton Corporation had bought from the Bennett-Stanford family of Preston Manor in 1883 to form Brighton's first public park. At the same time that the aquarium was needing a revamp, this other great Victorian development was also looking tired and so MacLaren, as Superintendent of Parks and Gardens, was tasked with devising a new scheme to impress residents and visitors entering Brighton who would pass by the park. MacLaren proposed lightening the park's brooding and dark Victorian feel, removing the heavy railings while demolishing the lodge at the southern end. The epicentre of his design was to be a massive 6-acre lake filling the side of the park parallel to London Road with a wealth of floral colour in an informal shape, and even having an island in the north-west corner 'where waterplants and reeds can grow and swans and waterfowl make their home'. Birds wouldn't be the only creatures to grace the lake, though, as Maclaren also envisaged the lake hosting regattas and watersport meetings. The weighty projected cost of £50,000 deterred further development and would have meant that the increasing demand for the park for football matches would have been affected. In the end, other projects were deemed more viable and important, but with the Wellesbourne flowing underneath the park to feed it 'Preston Lake' would have been a wildlife-friendly watery welcome to Brighton that sadly never was. Perhaps we need a statue to celebrate the visionary that was Captain Bertie Maclaren. Preston Park remains Brighton's biggest ornamental park and includes Britain's oldest velodrome in the north-east corner, which opened in 1877.

As the 1930s were followed by the Second World War, then the Cold War for the people of Sussex, threats to our shores changed from to Nazism to Communism and then terrorism. One Sussex hero from the end of the Cold War is not a person, or even an animal, but a piece of cloth. It is the Union Flag that flew every day for eighteen years above the Grand Hotel while manager Paul Boswell was in charge. It miraculously stayed flying proudly above the hotel despite the 1984 IRA bombing attack, which led to tons of masonry supporting the flag and flagpole beneath it crashing down, five people being killed and thirty-four injured on the terrible night of 12 October 1984. Somehow the flag remained, straddling part of the gaping hole caused by the collapse, but was eventually taken down on the orders of manager Paul Boswell.

The Metropole thankfully never faced a threat like the Grand, but it did experience its own unique threat back in the 1960s, providing us with an unlikely

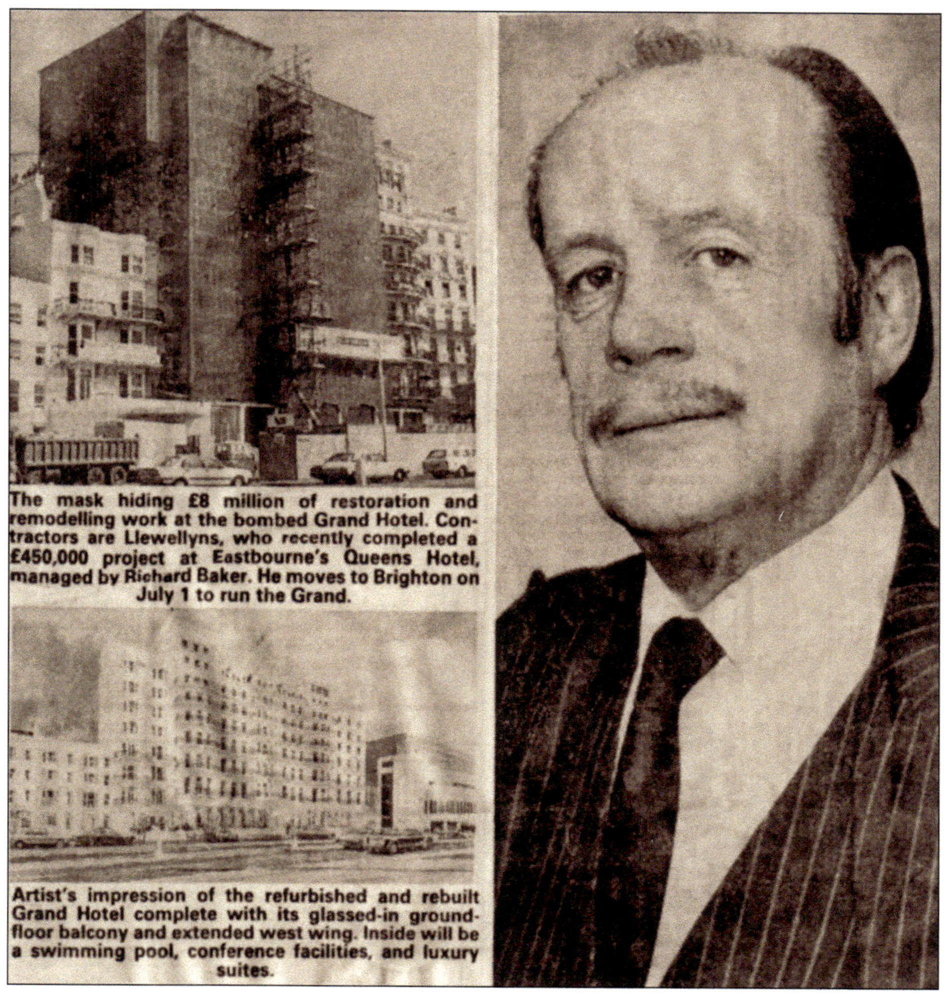

Paul Boswell and the Grand Hotel. (*The Argus*)

hero with a bucket. One of Brighton's biggest ever conferences was in February 1967 when the Ford Motor Company hosted a commercial vehicles conference in the Metropole's new exhibition halls. They decided to raise the excitement levels at its annual staff awards where there was a trip to Morocco as a prize for the top salesman. The company, thinking that Morocco equals camels, decided to bring a real-life camel named Sheena into the awards to increase excitement further. Unfortunately, Sheena never made it that far. Obviously sharing in the evening's excitement, she was unable to contain herself and decided to empty her bladder in the foyer of the exhibition at the Metropole. A quick-thinking general manager managed to save the honour of the hotel with quick reactions and a handy bucket!

From Africa to Asia. Yukio Kikuchi is not a name you would associate with Brighton, but he needs celebrating as the man whose love of Brighton means that the city is celebrated across Japan. The Japanese hotel boss visited Brighton in 1987 and met Jackie Lythell, Brighton's mayor back at the time. He was so impressed with both town and mayor that he decided to name his new six-floor, 183-room hotel in Kyoto after Brighton. The mayor of Brighton the following year, Pat Hawkes, and other council leaders were even invited by Mr Kukuchi over to Kyoto for the formal opening of the first of the chain of 'Brighton Hotels' in Japan, which was attended by over 1,500 guests. Today in Japan you can still have a little piece of Brighton in various Japanese locations due to the warm welcome Mr Kikuchi received and that a Japanese businessman fell in love with our city.

Mr Kukuchi is not the only fan of Brighton to name a place around the globe in the city's honour. There are at least forty-eight Brightons across the world, and Bristol, Bricklehampton, in Worcestershire and Brighthampton in Oxfordshire all started off with the same name. You can even find a Brighton south-east of Newquay if you go on holiday to Cornwall. Those with friends in Derbyshire might want to check out Brighton Farm, and anyone scouting about Scotland can check out another Brighton Farm near Fife. Unsurprisingly, we have the largest Brighton worldwide, with an Australian one 6 miles south of Melbourne coming in second with over 40,000 inhabitants. Australia has three other Brightons, but America has the greatest number of Brightons worldwide, with twenty-seven altogether and two in New York State and Ohio each. For somewhere made famous worldwide by a king (King George, as the Prince Regent eventually became), it is only right that Georgetown in Guyana has a Brighton to the south-east of it. The most southerly are in South Africa, New Zealand and Australia and the most northerly in Canada.

There are also Metropoles all over the world, but it was Brighton Metropole's former general manager Larry Duggan (died in 1989, at the age of just forty-seven) who was a hero to couples everywhere in the 1980s. Aware of the fact that couples on a 'dirty weekend' to Brighton often signed themselves into hotels as 'Mr and Mrs Smith', he promoted the idea that couples who actually did have that name could come to his hotels and get a 10 per cent discount. Real Smiths were also treated to sunglasses and fake moustaches for disguise, romantic perfume and a list of recommended romantic locations to visit. Duggan, who also had been manager of Hove's Imperial and Langfords hotels, had progressed by the time of his death to be managing director of firm Madkour Hotels, which also included Eastbourne's Burlington Hotel by 1989. His idea gained national publicity and his hotels gained enquiries from all over the world. Sadly, the man behind this heart-warming idea had a series of heart troubles and died from a coronary attack. As general manager of the Burlington, Gerard Mills, said at the time, 'He will be sadly missed.'

The 1990s were a tough time for the British pub industry according to local newspaper reports of the time. The situation was finally helped in the late 1990s by the deregulation of Sunday drinking and longer licensing laws. It seems hard to believe that only twenty-five years ago foreign visitors to Britain were mystified by our licensing laws. Most strange to our eyes now, pubs then had to close or stop serving beer halfway through the 1995 Rugby World Cup match between England and New Zealand. One Brighton village fought back at this tricky time when its historic pub was threatened with demolition and replacement with a restaurant, motel and parking for 200 cars. The Plough in Pyecombe, north of Brighton, was a target for development by the owners, Whitbread, due to its ideal location next to the busy A23. The villagers united behind the parish council in an energetic campaign involving petitions, letter writing and getting key individuals – from councillors to MPs – on board. The planning application was rejected by Mid Sussex District Council, proving that a determined small village could win against big business, and thanks to these heroes the Plough is still successfully running today.

Brighton and Hove's Black History Group (BAHBHG) has been brought to the public's attention and publicised due to the work of Brighton hero Bert Williams, who was honoured in 2011 with an MBE for his work. Bert has been the driving force behind Brighton and Hove Black History Group, which was formally started in 2002, and since then has spent much of his retirement researching and presenting the multicultural history of the city. Before that he was a member of the RAF until 1967 when he moved to Brighton to work for the NHS. The group are now involved with many projects, such as 'Time and Place', which has researched the lives of nurses who came to Brighton from Britain's former colonies. It tells of a range of experiences, from the 1960s nurse who experimented with a 'Twiggy' haircut to the nurses couldn't get to an Afro-Caribbean hairdresser in London so they would try straightening their hair using a stove.

The BAHBHG website also tells of the range of black, Asian and heroes from many other minority or ethnic groups involved in law and order over the centuries. Henry Solomon, an active member of Brighton's synagogue, was also Brighton's first Jewish chief constable in the 1830s. He was sadly murdered in 1844 when left alone with a suspect. The four daughters of the Wells family moved to Brighton in the 1880s. Their father was Nathaniel Wells (b. 1779), a very early Justice of the Peace despite his background as the son of a slave and Welsh merchant. Moving into the twenty-first century, Cheryl Marsh was one of Sussex Police's members who made a huge difference. She was instrumental in getting domestic violence training for other PCSOs implemented across the city. She sadly died in 2007 of asbestosis.

Another Brighton hero who died the year before – 2006 – was celebrated in 2019 by becoming one of the names given to Brighton and Hove's buses. Jacky Harding, who died from liver failure at the tragic young age of forty-five, arrived in 1969 as eight-year-old Sierra Leone. At that time Brighton had very few ethnic minority residents and discrimination was an issue. This didn't deter Jacky, who not only advocated but also demonstrated how education could change lives. She enrolled at Sussex University as an economics student and dedicated her time to promoting lifelong education for all people. She achieved this by working for the University of Brighton and also being a founder member of the Learning and Skills Council of Sussex. She also set out to educate peoples' political views as well as help and represent others through joining the Labour Party and becoming a community worker. Described as a true barrier-breaker, in 2000 Jacky became the first black woman to be elected to Brighton and Hove City Council for Labour. With her personal experience of how education could transform the lives of ethnic minorities, she was made lead councillor for the Labour group on lifelong learning. Jacky, despite her short life, still demonstrates how education matters and reminds us that Brighton and Hove is, and has been, a city of opportunities.

Henry Allingham, who died in 2009, was one of our last First World War veterans who made it to the rare category of supercentenarian (someone over 110) and for one month was the oldest man in the world. Henry served as an air mechanic in the Royal Naval Air Service, predecessor of the Fleet Air Arm. During his time in the RNAS in 1916 Allingham participated in the Battle of Jutland as an air mechanic in HMS *Kingfisher*. He would be the last survivor from either side. He also served on land, experiencing a shell hole full of decaying bodies at the Third Battle of Ypres (Passchendaele) in 1917. He moved to St Dunstan's care home in Ovingdean in 2006 at the age of 109 and died there in 2009 at the age of 113. He is commemorated by Brighton and Hove Bus No. 808.

From death to life. To educate us today in Sussex about matters of eggs and birds, we have the fantastic Macmillan family. The 'Macs' (as they are known) write for *Sussex Life* each month on egg matters and have one of the eco-friendliest egg farms in the country in Ditchling. Not only do all their elderly layers go on to good homes courtesy of Patcham's RSPCA (over 75,000 to count), but they are a fourth-generation organic-egg-farming family who really love what they do. Back in 1994 Grandma and Grandpa Mac were one of the first ever suppliers of free-range eggs to the major supermarkets. As a sign of their success, their farm that once consisted of one shed that was used for pig farming, has now been organic for twenty years and today has four chicken sheds with 18,000 organic free-range birds (or 'girls' as the Macs call them). The Macs are amazing as they open up their farm every day of the year, champion pullet eggs (which are too small for supermarkets), have taken on the might of Tesco and, most importantly, have made sure 75,000 birds ended their days in friendly chicken coops rather than being destroyed.

Our most recent of Brighton heroes, though, must be the academic behind a 2019 *Argus* story with the headline 'Older Women Are Having Disappointing Sex Lives'. This was the report that explained Brighton University's research showed that only a third of post-menopausal women were sexually active and that 40.5 per cent of these women's lack of sex was down to their partner's medical conditions or sexual dysfunction. The academic behind the study was the wonderfully named Dr Helena Harder.

Sussex has two universities in Brighton, meaning that a number of worthies, celebrities and famous people spent their time studying here. Firstly, there's Matthew Dent, who designed the current images on our coins, so you carry his work around with you. Brighton University was the home to Andrew Goodall, chief executive of Brighton Marina, and John Pasche, who designed the tongue and lips logo for the Rolling Stones. The university has championed musical talent too, with Natasha Khan (Bat for Lashes) and Orlando Weeks from the Maccabees attending. Billy Idol started his secondary schooling at Worthing High and ended at Sussex University, as did Labour grandee Hilary Benn. On the topic of politics, Guy Scott, the temporary Prime Minister of Ghana, studied here in Sussex as did comedian Frankie Boyle. Bob Mortimer studied here in his days before teaming up with Vic Reeves, and Fat Boy Slim (Norman Cook) was right here, right then at university too. Radio 2's Jo Whiley also spent here university days here, studying applied language. Put them all together and it would have made an interesting student union bar!

Our final hero is also in the field of education: an eleven-year-old boy who did something amazing back in 1925, a time when often those in positions of responsibility were suffering from the mental and physical exertions of their time in the trenches in the First World War. One such person was Michael (Mick) O'Byrne, better known as 'MOB', who became the first headmaster of Claremont School, which was established in 1925 in Hove's Second Avenue. The school is the setting of my historical novel, *Beef Every Day But No Latin*.

MOB became headteacher following the persuasion of a remarkable eleven-year-old boy called James Bernard Clifton who decided to start up the Claremont School after his maths teacher at his previous school (Holland House) threw a maths book at his head. James, who would have been five when the war ended, was proof that the war may have damaged the country irreparably, but young minds could still dream and achieve. Britain never again achieved the wealth or worldwide status it had before the First World War, but this generation produced men such as James (or 'Clifton' as he was known) who went on to be an inventor and engineer and would ensure Britain didn't lose a much bigger world conflict in 1939. Clifton's inventions carried on into the Cold War and even helped Britain's efforts in the Space Race. They live on today, as does the Claremont School, which survives today in East Sussex despite its Hove home being bombed in the Second World War.

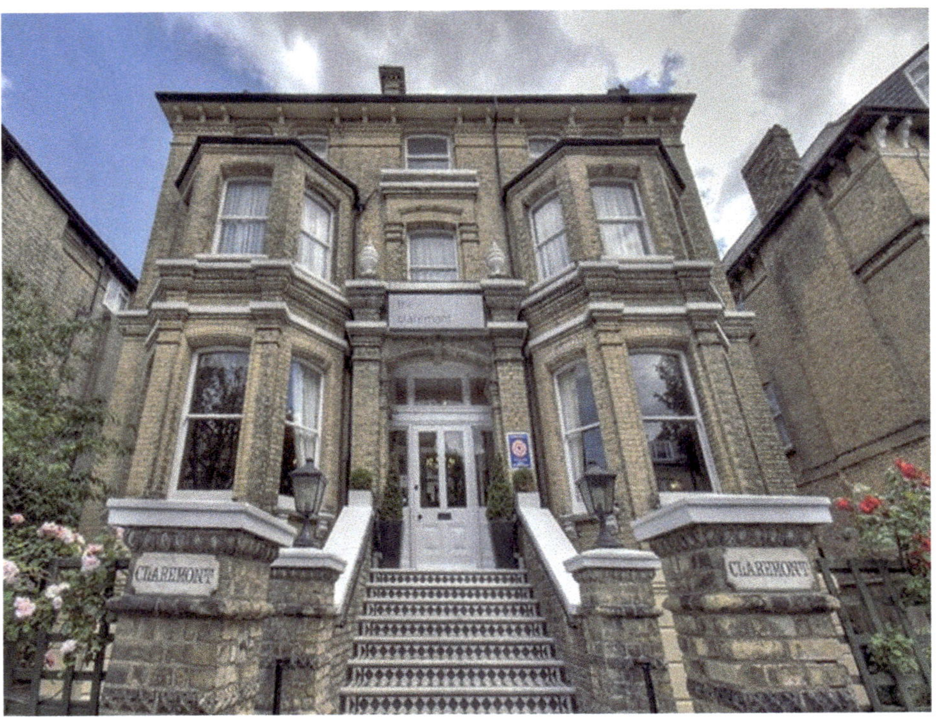

The Claremont Guest House, site of Claremont School.

MOB didn't last long as headmaster, unfortunately. He was in terrible physical and mental pain and his alcoholism led to rapid mental decline, which mean his son William O'Byrne had to take over the school while still a teenager. Bill (or 'WOB' as he was known) dedicated his life to the school through the Second World War and died young in the 1950s for his efforts. His children naturally missed having their father around and soon lost their home – the school – afterwards.

And so, this is just one Sussex example as to how the impact of the First World War didn't stop neatly at 11 o'clock on 11 November 1918, but would still be felt down the generations. As we have seen, though, not all of the impacts of the war were detrimental. But most were. Even with the Claremont School (and you can visit it today as it is the The Claremont in Second Avenue, Hove), it is an example of the hardship that followed war in the 1920s, but also of the next generation who carried on and still achieved great things. Perhaps without the experiences in the trenches the teacher who threw the book at Clifton's head might never have done so. The teachers of the 1920s were the veterans of the First World War. Typically a nervous, haggard, aged but yet unbeaten generation whose lives would never be the same, and were often shorter because of that horrific war.

Are you wondering who that teacher was who threw the book at Clifton? Well, it was none other than Mick O' Byrne, who Clifton then went on to persuade to become his school's first headteacher. Why would a boy ask a teacher who threw a book at him to lead the school he set up? Well, that's another story for another day.

Local Traditions

With the sea to the south and the Downs to the north, Brighton is an auditorium of exciting adventures, some of which are long overdue a return. Today we enjoy paddling around the pier and burning the clocks, but Brighton has also experienced the Prince Regent's octogenarian race, Lord Bullock's beating of Barrymore and the famous 'Patcham Fawcett School Gob Pit'. Brighton even has its own lingo: if you're having your 'pitcher' taken, this has nothing to do with cameras, instead someone is robbing you of your housebuilding material – it means a flint. Brighton's famously prestigious girls' school Roedean also once had its own slang: if you 'visited auntie' there you wouldn't get a hug or boiled sweets, as it meant that you were going to the toilet. Other slang there including you eating a 'burned baby's arm', which thankfully was only a pudding, as was 'Thames mud'. Sussex apparently is unusual for having a large number of words for mud. A 'keenie' was a younger girl at Roedean who had a crush on an older one.

Our traditions are not just on land. The Old Ship in Brighton is to thank for an amazing annual yacht race every year from Brighton to France with historical provenance. The Royal Escape Race started back in 1976 when Linda Morgan, the PR officer for Brighton's Old Ship Hotel called the Sussex Yacht Club, had the idea for a race across the Channel. Linda was apparently very passionate about the idea and wanted to see every yacht in Sussex on the starting line. She took some calming down to recognise that with the limited facilities then available perhaps it should be scaled down a bit to just include SYC yachts, but the event has since grown and takes place every year in May. The Old Ship was still heavily involved back in the 1990s and used to fire the starting cannon for the race from its rooftop.

Edward the Confessor, Henry VIII, Thomas Cromwell, Anne of Cleves and secretary Jackie Aistrop all have one thing in common. Two of them might not have been the best of husbands, but Jackie's claim to fame in 1988 wasn't that. They had all at some point continued the local tradition of owning the title 'Lord of the Manor of Brighton'. The lucky lady won the title in a competition organised by the *Evening Standard* newspaper. Jackie had one small problem, though: the fifty-two-year-old lived in a flat 50 miles away in London. To further reduce the glamour of the prize, she was only allowed to use the title on her stationery, passport and coat of arms. Like most fifty-two-year-old secretaries, she unsurprisingly didn't have a coat of arms!

The 1990s saw a new event occur at the Grand Hotel each May with a much-missed name. The Big Dangle took place down the side of the illustrious hotel every year, and in 1997 *The Argus* reported on the 100 abseilers, all of whom raised a projected £10,000 for the Imperial Cancer Research Fund (Cancer Research UK today) by abseiling the 100-foot drop. The following year Eddie 'the Eagle' Edwards helped publicise the event and the target was raised to £25,000.

The Children's Festival is a fantastic annual Brighton event and a time we don't mind the streets being closed down to traffic and all the associated delays as it means our kids can safely exhibit their best costumes, show pride in their schools and make lots of noise (as well as make people happy). It managed to cause the biggest tailback of Brighton and Hove buses ever in the days before the services got rerouted; North Street was a huge mass of red and cream as the buses were all back to back. Managed by Same Sky, a community arts organisation who also run the Burning the Clocks event, it is great to see the children take over the Lanes and North Laine and proudly march with their classmates, teachers and parents, dressed up in a plethora of wonderful costumes.

Making great music and hosting great musicians is definitely a wonderful Brighton tradition. The sadly defunct Hippodrome in Brighton hosted the Rolling Stones and the Beatles, which is reason alone to support its much-needed current restoration plans. In the 1970s, Sussex was home to 'Phun City', the UK's first large-scale free music festival. In 1974 the Eurovision Song Contest took place at the Dome, which propelled ABBA to worldwide fame. Major festivals include the Great Escape Festival and Glyndebourne Festival Opera.

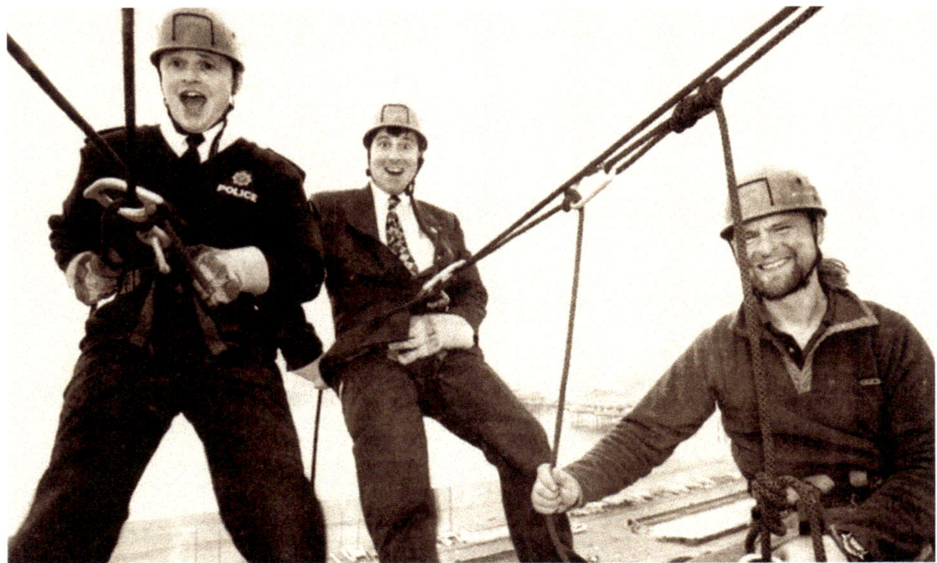

The Big Dangle. (*The Argus*)

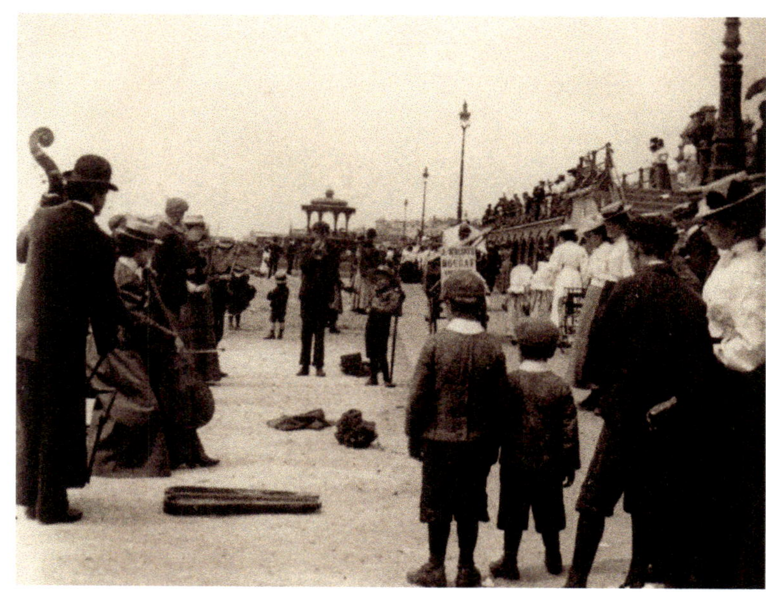

Victorian musicians performing by King's Road.

Nearby Shorehan has produced artists including Leo Sayer (who wrote the song 'Moonlighting', which features Worthing's Montague Street), and The Levellers, The Cure, Brett Anderson, Keane, The Kooks, The Feeling, Rizzle Kicks, Conor Maynard, Tom Odell and Royal Blood are all from Brighton, nearby or have links. As mentioned before Kylie Minogue played her first live performance in Britain at the Metropole in the 1980s, Fat Boy Slim is practically Brighton royalty, and James Bay was a student here at the British and Irish Modern Music Institute (BIMM). Mastermind behind the musical hall of fame between Concorde II and the Palace Pier, David Courtney said of Brighton, 'Brighton is a pioneering place for so many things, but it's always been a hotbed of music.' Courtney would know as he worked with Shoreham superstar Leo Sayer back in the 1970s and said, 'Outside London you would be hard-pressed to find somewhere with so many names attached to it.' Lastly, Chesney Hawkes once performed his hit 'The One And Only' at the Odeon in Brighton in the 1990s to at least a dozen screaming teenage girls.

Brighton is the beard capital of the UK according to the British Beard Club, which has its headquarters in Brighton. Typical of our bohemian city in the centre of Sussex, Brighton has gone against the findings in a new study that claims more than nine in ten women do not like men with beards. As reported in *The Argus*, half of women surveyed told a cosmetics firm they preferred their other halves clean-shaven, with 94 per cent saying they would avoid kissing a man with a full beard. We would hope for no less from a county that has a beard products company named after it in Canada. The Sussex Beard Oil Merchants sell their products around the world and its founder has even appeared on the Canadian version of *Dragon's Den*. You could even once 'drink Beards' in Brighton, but this is no more. Sussex sadly lost Beard's Brewery in 1999 when it was bought by Greene King, but a Beards Brewery still exists – in Missouri, USA.

Pageants, Fairs, Festivals and Fun

E. V. Lucas in 1904 tells of how Brighton could once 'lay before her guests a thousand odd diversions,' and this was in addition to her 'concerts, balls, masquerades, theatres [and] races'. The epicentre of entertainment was the Steine, which was once 'an arena for curious contests'. Lucas tells of how 'officers and gentlemen, ridden by other officers and gentlemen competed in races with octogenarians. Strapping young women were induced to run against each other for a new smock or hat'. He continues, 'Every kind of race was devised, even to walking backwards; while a tame stag was occasionally liberated and hunted to refuge.' Apart from the animal cruelty, how much fun would it be to have a 'Brighton Alternative Olympics' once more.

Brighton Festival is known worldwide today and is the biggest and most established annual multi-arts festival in England. Established in 1967, it's known

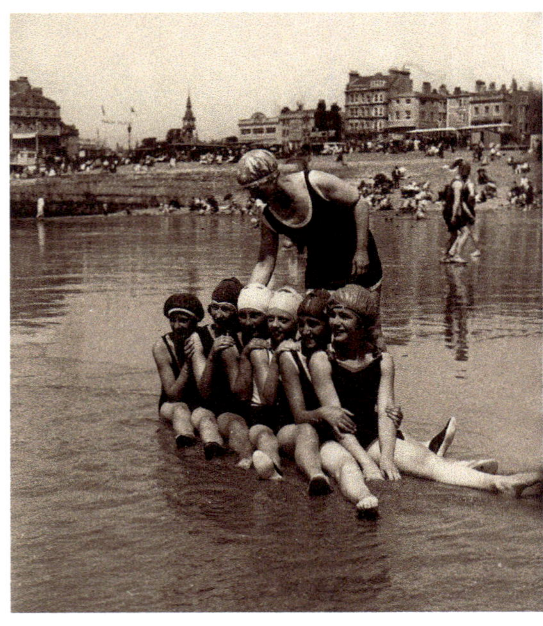

Girls on the beach having fun.

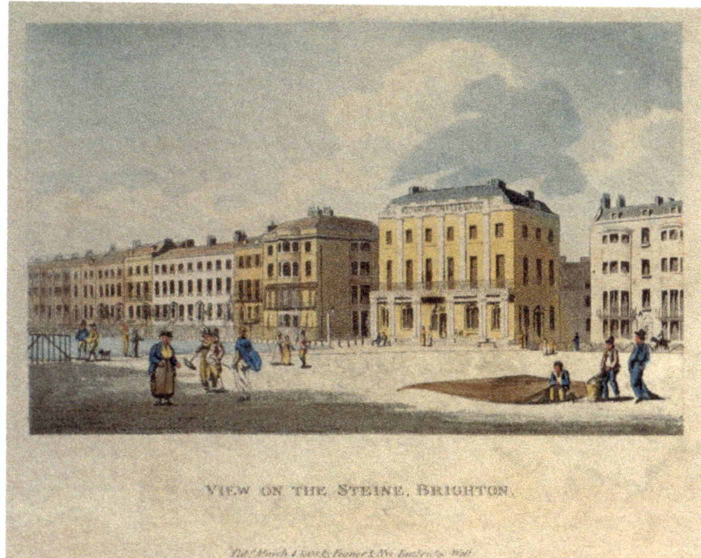

Right: View on the Steine, Brighton, 1808.

Below: Brighton's past performers.

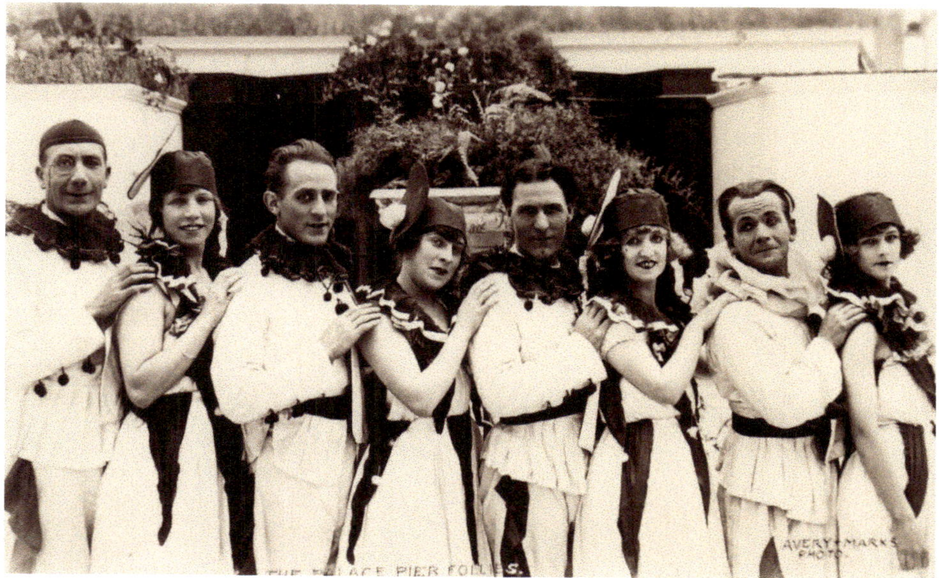

for its ambitious and daring programme that aims to make the most of the city's distinctive cultural atmosphere, drawing some of the most innovative artists and companies from the UK and around the world. However, its path to its current successful status hasn't always been a smooth one. Today it celebrates all that is creative about the city with a range of events late into the night, but in 1987 the magistrates and police of Brighton seemed set on a spectacular snub. Festival sites applied for late licences but were turned down by the courts, who were advised by the police that they 'did not consider that the Festival was a special event', according to Phil Grainger, licensee of the Colonnade in New Road. The festival is known today for its green credentials, so it is unlikely its organisers would try to recreate the publicity stunt they undertook in its inaugural year back in 1967. An attempt to draw a Union Jack on the sea between the piers led to the colours merging to make a murky green mess.

With our Assembly Rooms, exhibition suites, dance floors and ballrooms past and present it is no wonder Brighton was – and is – known as a place to celebrate. With two universities and the Greater Brighton Metropolitan College residing in the city, it is not surprising these celebrations are often educational in their nature. One of these such events was the Sussex University Engineers' Ball, which back in 1997 used the services of a most unusual limousine for three of its female students. The story starts with media student Katherine Salt joking at The Bear in Lewes Road where she worked as a barmaid. She laughed that she and two friends, Rachel Hamm and Danielle Nugent, had spent so much money on their ballgowns that they couldn't afford a taxi and would have to travel in a dustcart. Local dustman Tony McLenahan, who worked at the depot over the road from the Bear, offered to take the three students up on the joke and actually use his dustcart as a limo. He gained permission from his bosses at Ecovert South and delivered the three glamourous students from the Bear to the Grand.

Eleven years earlier, *The Argus* reported on a lady who had gone one step further. Hove estate agent Joanna Smith won a £50 bet when her friend in the Plough of Rottingdean criticised what she was wearing and dared her to come

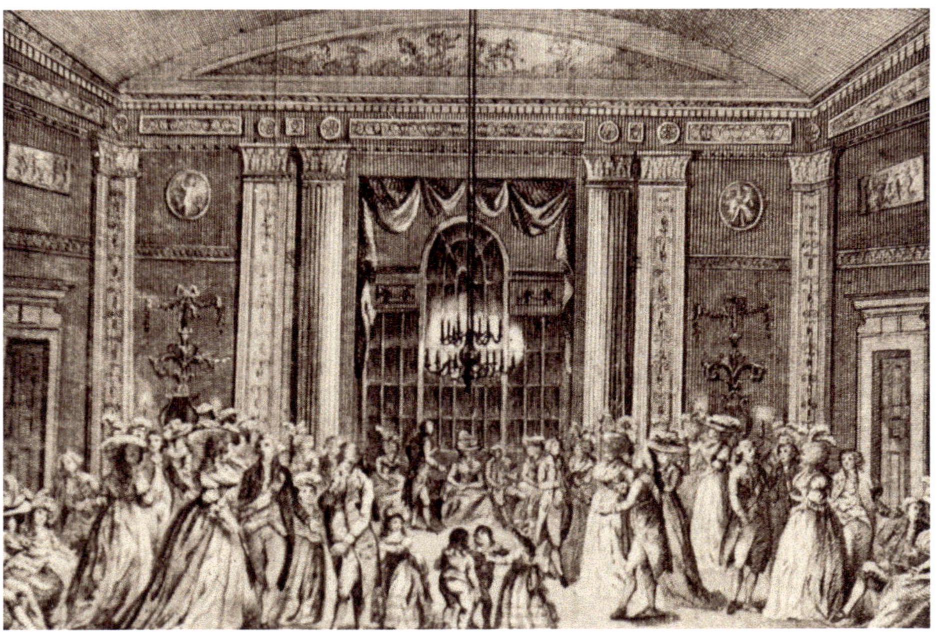

Assembly Room, The Castle Hotel.

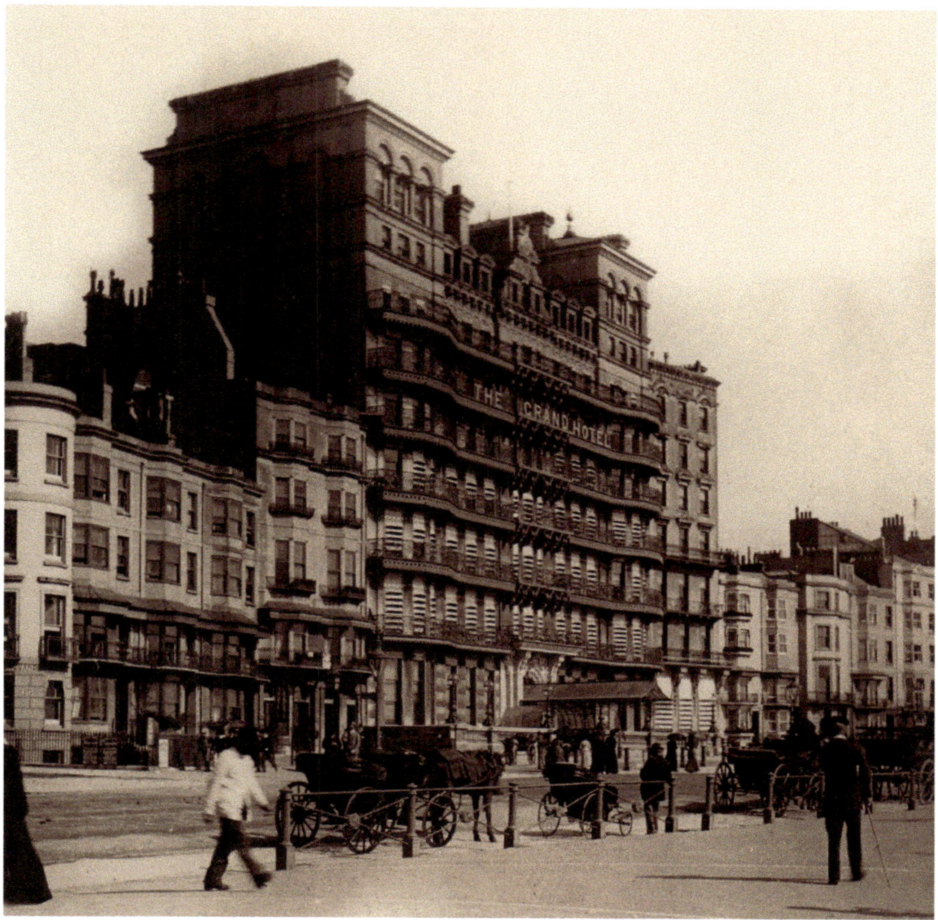

The Grand Hotel.

into the pub wearing nothing but a black bin liner. Not only did she take him up on the bet, but she collected a further £70 and donated the lot to Cancer Research and the RNLI.

Bin liners and dustcarts are what we used to take away our unwanted household waste, but the bizarre unwanted items left behind in Brighton's hotels are worth celebrating for their weirdness. Back in 1997, Brighton's Grand Hotel was left with an inflatable woman and a wooden leg. Not by the same person, though. 'The inflatable doll was left by a couple,' explained the Grand's deputy manager at the time, Robert Allen. 'The wooden leg turned out to be a spare,' said Allen, 'so thankfully it wasn't needed as urgently as we thought and the chap who left it did eventually claim it.' The Grand was also left with a 'stuffed ferret and a range of antiques'. Brighton's Norfolk hotel, (today the Mercure Brighton Seafront Hotel) was left with 'a bag of saucy ladies' underwear, left by a single man, who didn't call back to claim it', according to manager Ann Hancock.

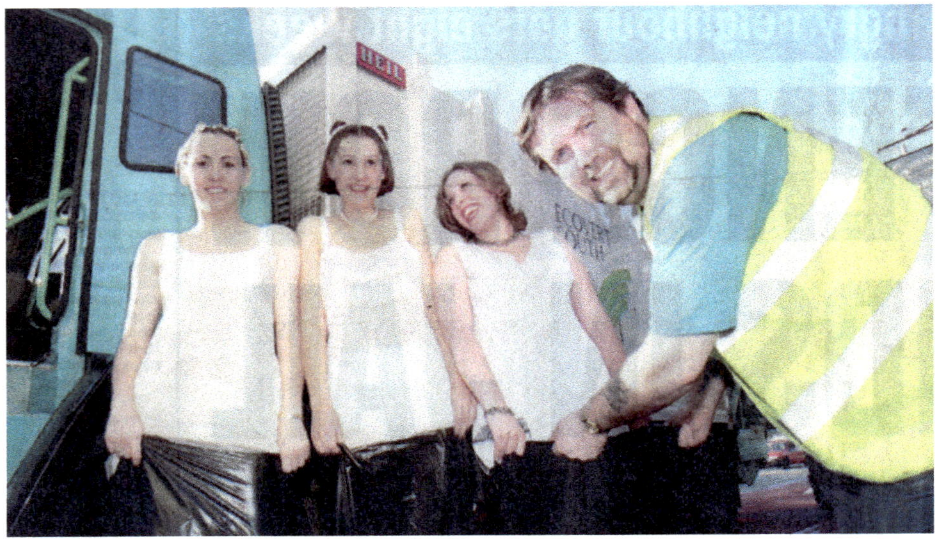

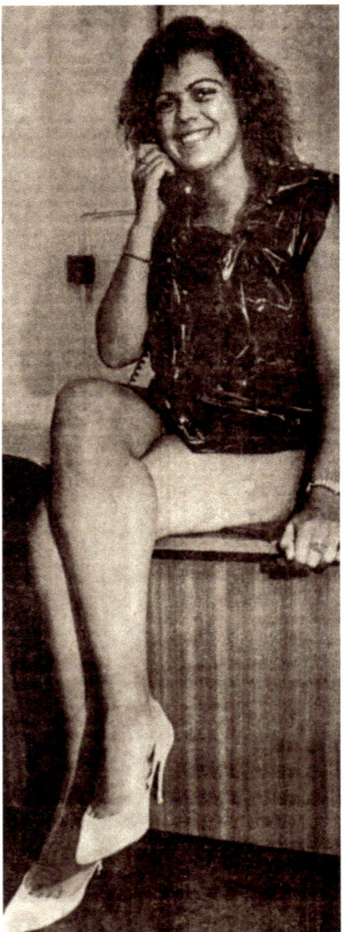

Above: Engineering students with an unusual limo for their ball. (*The Argus*)

Left: Joanna Smith. (*The Argus*)

11

Royal Visits

Brighton has been visited by countless numbers of royals. The first documented British royal to visit the town was Charles II when he was on the run from the Parliamentarians in the Civil War in 1651 – nine years before being restored as king. It is thought he stayed where the Travelodge is now on West Street. The 1750s were when the first royals came here to enjoy Brighton as a seaside resort, starting with the dukes of Gloucester and then Cumberland, the latter of which was the uncle of the future George IV. George enjoyed escaping his father's stuffy court so much in 1783 that he took up residence the following year, going on to revamp his residence from 1821 to make it into our current Royal Pavilion.

Prince (and later King) George may have brought wealth and fame to the town, but it came at a price for those responsible for his security and safety. The leading male 'dipper' Smoaker Miles once risked the Prince Regent's fury by refusing to let

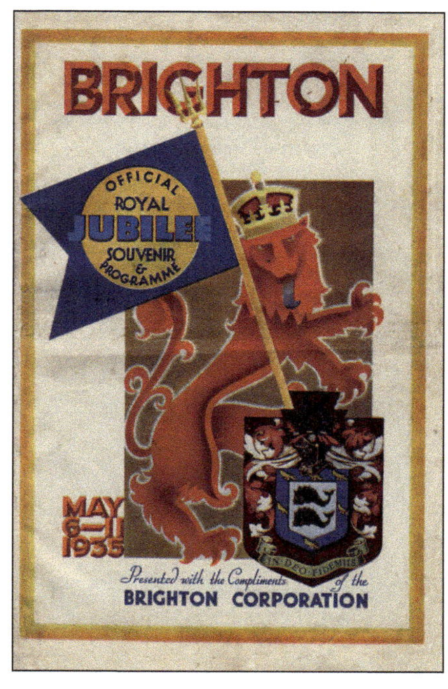

Programme of a royal persuasion.

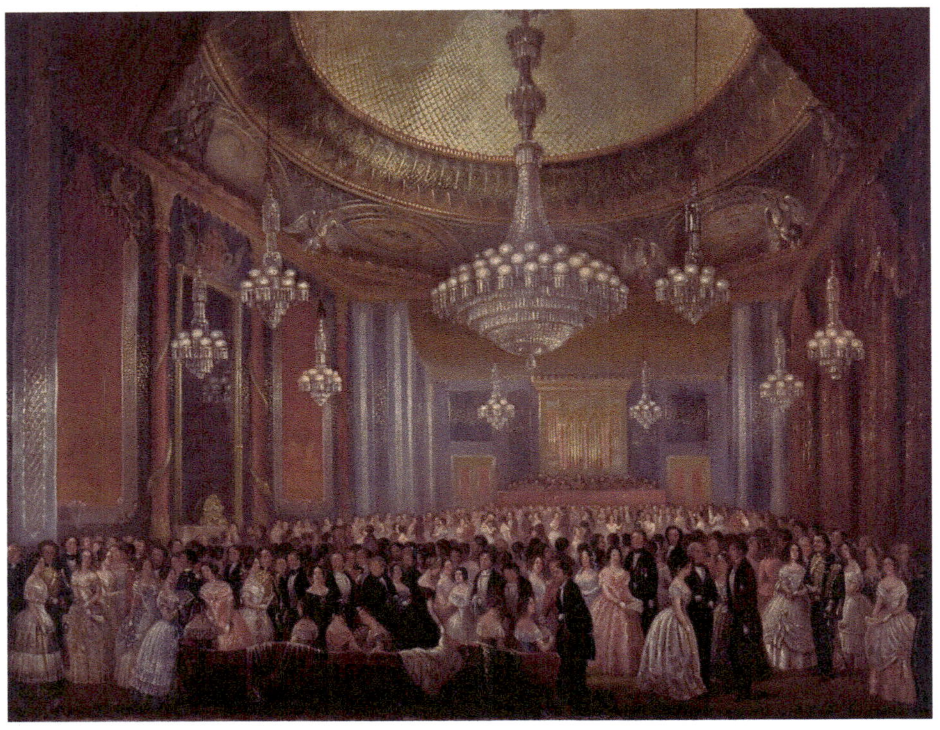

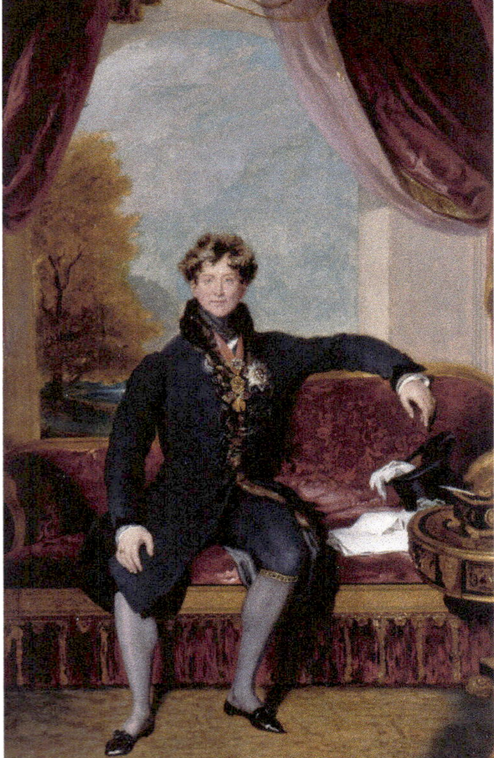

Above: The Royal Pavilion.

Left: George seated by Sir Thomas Lawrence in the nineteenth century.

him take a swim in the sea as the waves were too strong. The prince, fortunately, was good natured about his reproach. Princely protocols even led to injuries and death for common folk. George's first ever visit in 1783, to stay with his uncle, was celebrated with a royal salute from the town's gun battery; however, one of the guns misfired, blasting the artillery soldier's body who had fired the cannon down onto the beach. His hand was blown clear from his body into the sea and was never found. Strangely, another similar salute for George's baby sister Amelia a year earlier also led to another gunner also losing a hand, but fortunately he survived. So it wasn't just taxpayers' wallets the royals hurt. The royals didn't even need to be in town for deaths to occur. In rushing to get the first version of the Pavilion (the Marine Pavilion) ready for George's visit, a terrible accident occurred to the workmen rushing to complete the original building's glass dome in time. Thankfully, George IV's younger brother's (William IV) time in Brighton seems a lot less dangerous, with Benevolent Billy content to give out sweets to children when walking on the Chain Pier.

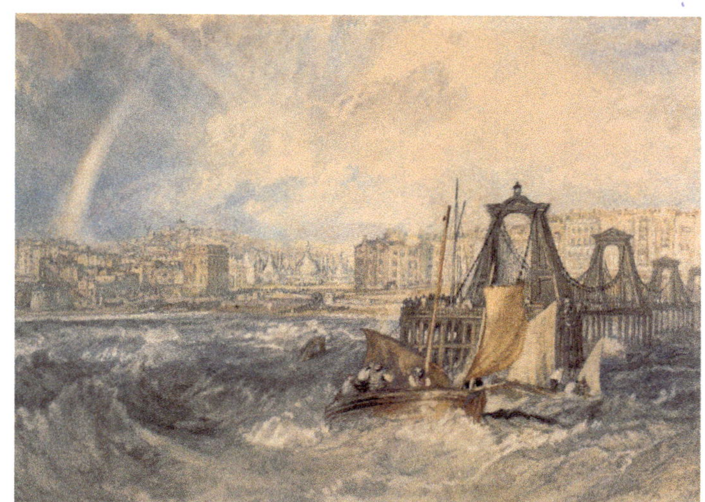

Right: A watercolour by JMW Turner of Brighthelmston, Sussex, *c.* 1824.

Below: Race meeting.

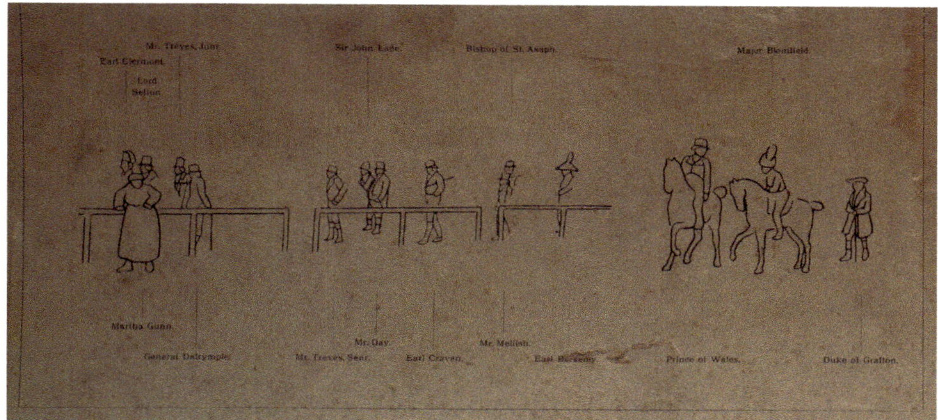

Brighton Racecourse has roots back over 300 years. The Duke of Richmond and his fellow racing fans helped create the first races, which also brought more of the earliest visitors to the town. Horses were being raced unofficially on the Downs at Whitehawk as far back as before 1713, before our earliest tourists (we have letters from Revd William Clarke in 1736). It was not until 1783, however, that the Duke of Cumberland organised the first official race at the area of White Hawk Down, or 'Race Hill' as it became known. Aristocratic participants kept their horses in the town, the grandest of all being Prince George who, in building his Indian-style stables and training centre (the Dome, Museum and Corn Exchange today) in 1805, admitted his horses lived in grander buildings than he did, thus copying the style of those buildings for the final incarnation of the Pavilion. So, we can confidently say that horses helped the Royal Pavilion to be built. The prince was hooked from the second-ever official meeting in 1784, as were many other nobles. Brighton boomed due to its racecourse, so we must thank horses as much perhaps as Hanoverian monarchs like George IV and his brother William for Brighton booming. A wonderful tale is that it was these turf-loving toffs who created the idea of steeplechases in Brighton by training their horses to leap over sheep pens as the first ever hurdles in racing.

Brighton may never have hosted the Olympics, but we did host two matches of the 2015 Rugby World Cup, and we did once host our very own odd 'food olympics' of events in 1820 when George, the Prince Regent, became King George IV on George III's death. The coronation poster advertised not just a '63-gun salute', but also a range of seemingly meat-themed events (perhaps a secret message as to 'Georgie Porgey's' weight by this time). These included the 'chasing of pigs with a soaked tail' to win the pig, 'climbing up a greasy pole' to win some meat, and the drinking of pints of beer, aptly, in ten hogsheads. Food included the 'cutting up of an oxen' for distribution to all. Fittingly, the music to accompany this meat marathon was the song 'Roast Beef of Old England'.

The Pavilion is Brighton's most well-known building, but that doesn't stop it having several secrets we don't know the answers to. There are two voids where nothing exists within the building – presumably leftover spaces from when Prince George ordered the removal of the east wings during one of its makeovers. We still don't know where the prince's Chinese lantern room was, and the building today is only a fraction of its total size at its biggest state as many of the southern rooms and kitchens were demolished. Two buildings, one of which was Brighton's huge Castle Inn, were demolished to allow it to expand; at its heart is still a lowly Brighton farmhouse. The staircases are constructed of fake bamboo, as George thought metal handrails too cold. George hated the cold so the palace was always kept unbearably hot, with working class men below ground keeping the furnaces going and small boys forced to climb up 9-inch-wide chimneys in scary conditions to clean the chimneys. The Pavilion was a place of pain as well as pleasure. Most mysteriously though are four holes in the kitchen. The Pavilion's kitchen was steam-powered, and it is believed these holes contained steam pipes to heat hotplates or other paraphernalia.

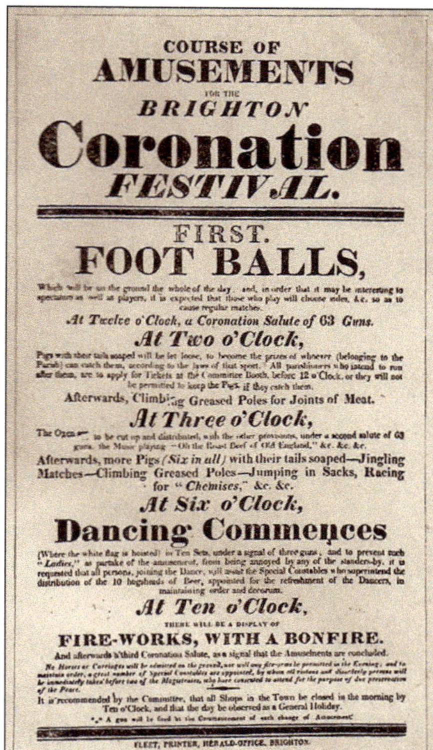

COURSE OF
AMUSEMENTS
FOR THE
BRIGHTON
Coronation
FESTIVAL.

FIRST.
FOOT BALLS,

Which will be on the ground the whole of the day; and, in order that it may be interesting to spectators as well as players, it is expected that those who play will choose sides, &c. so as to cause regular matches.

At Twelve o'Clock, a Coronation Salute of 63 Guns.
At Two o'Clock,

Pigs with their tails soaped will be let loose, to become the prizes of whoever (belonging to the Parish) can catch them, according to the laws of that sport. All parishioners who intend to run after them, are to apply for Tickets at the Committee Booth, before 12 o'Clock, or they will not be permitted to keep the Pigs, if they catch them.

Afterwards, Climbing Greased Poles for Joints of Meat.
At Three o'Clock,

The Oxen to be cut up and distributed, with the other provisions, under a second salute of 63 guns, the Music playing "Oh the Roast Beef of Old England," &c. &c. &c.

Afterwards, more Pigs *(Six in all)* with their tails soaped—Jingling Matches—Climbing Greased Poles—Jumping in Sacks, Racing for "*Chemises,*" &c. &c.
At Six o'Clock,
Dancing Commences

(Where the white flag is hoisted) in Ten Sets, under a signal of three guns; and to prevent such "*Ladies,*" as partake of the amusement, from being annoyed by any of the standers-by, it is requested that all persons, joining the Dance, will assist the Special Constables who superintend the distribution of the 10 hogsheads of Beer, appointed for the refreshment of the Dancers, in maintaining order and decorum.
At Ten o'Clock,
THERE WILL BE A DISPLAY OF
FIRE-WORKS, WITH A BONFIRE.

And afterwards a third Coronation Salute, as a signal that the Amusements are concluded.

No Horses or Carriages will be admitted on the ground, nor will any fire-arms be permitted in the Evening; and to maintain order, a great number of Special Constables are appointed, by whom all violent and disorderly persons will be immediately taken before one of the Magistrates, who have consented to attend for the purpose of due preservation of the Peace.

It is recommended by the Committee, that all Shops in the Town be closed in the morning by Ten o'Clock, and that the day be observed as a General Holiday.

*** A gun will be fired at the Commencement of each change of Amusement.*

FLEET, PRINTER, HERALD-OFFICE, BRIGHTON.

Right: Coronation poster.

Below: The Pavilion's kitchen.

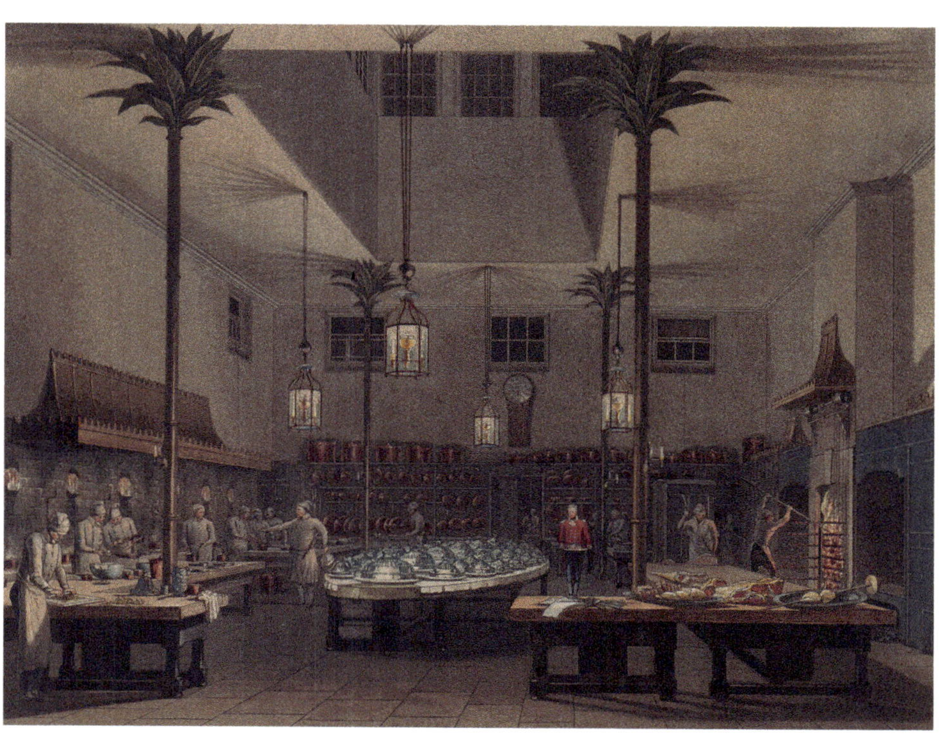

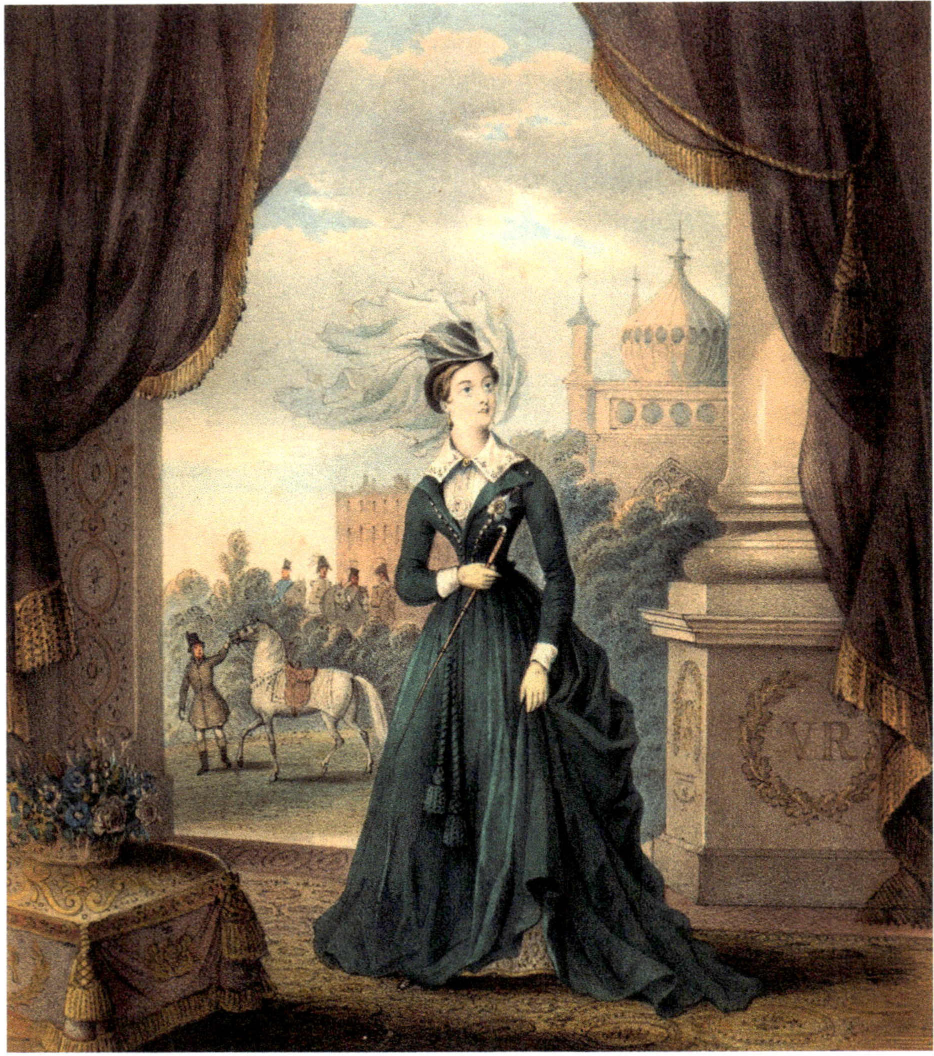

Queen Victoria with the Royal Pavilion in the background, *c.* 1840.

Brighton is known for being a place where romantic couples come for a weekend away. Even T. S. Eliot, in his poem 'The Wasteland', talks about the author being offered a weekend at the Metropole. However, Brighton has an unusual claim to fame for having two certain people stay together at the same time. It is probably the only place in the country that has ever had a current prime minister and monarch have residences in the same time period. Both George IV and his prime minister, George Canning, had homes here in 1827. It is a pretty safe bet to say that they didn't need to share a hotel room.

Queen Victoria's relationship with Brighton is a strange one, but she doesn't deserve the acrimonious press she has received from some local historians. Victoria never visited the Royal Pavilion until four months after she became queen as her uncle, William IV, didn't get on well with Victoria's mother, the Duchess of Kent. Alexandrina Victoria, as she was actually called, deserves some celebration just for having such a dreadful name alone. Firstly, her leaving us didn't do that much harm. All our biggest and grandest hotels (the Norfolk, Grand and Metropole) were built *after* she deserted us, as visitor numbers to Brighton continued to boom along with our other seaside resorts throughout her reign. We gained the grandest of all function rooms, exhibition suites, civic halls and today a world-famous museum and palace. Most Brightonians and millions of visitors this century alone have explored what, without Victoria's actions, may still be a private building today. No longer having a royal residence here meant that visiting royals actually had to do what the rest of us did and pay to book into a hotel (usually the Bedford) from the 1840s. We also got the Pavilion for a snip at £53,000, 10 per cent of what it cost to build, and a fraction of the millions of pounds it has made the town (and now city) since then. Victoria chipped in to build Brighton churches (Christ Church and St John's the Evangelist, since you ask) and also gave her blessing to people of all classes having seaside holidays. This meant resorts like Brighton boomed with the arrival of railways. She was the last of the Hanoverians, the family without whom Brighton would never have developed as it did. Brighton benefitted from her presence in many ways and so it is only fitting therefore that Hanover is one of our most popular and booming

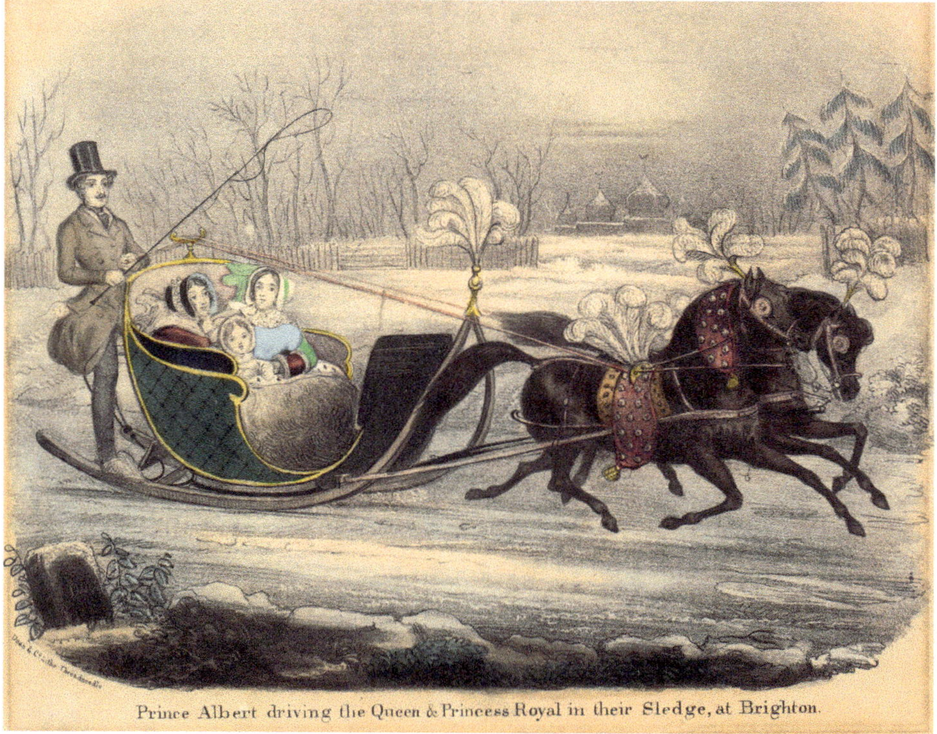

Prince Albert driving the queen and Princess Royal.

Brighton areas to live today. And, if you're a republican, at least she and Albert never conceived more children here (I've checked the dates!) whose descendants would be adding to the number of royal hangers-on today.

The most unusual royal visit must be the King of Morocco, who took over the whole of the Grand Hotel when he visited. Bill Dummett, doorman at the hotel in 1997, told *The Argus* how the monarch brought his own staff and, even more amazingly, his own bed. Despite all the preparations he only stayed for one night. The Princess of Thailand was also another 1990s visitor, but a century before the Metropole seems to have had the prize for the greatest number of royal visitors. From the Victorian era alone until the 1950s we were in the presence of a marquess, marquesses, dukes, duchesses, kings-to-be and at least sixteen of our own royals. Moving on to the aristocracy, the Metropole's guest list for 1890 alone reads like a dinner party at Downton Abbey. It includes the Countesse of Stradbrooke, Lady Gwendoline Rous, the Honourable Charles Willoughby, Sir Jasper Carmichael, the Comtesse du Bremont, and not to forget the wonderfully named Count Appongi. Brighton's most exotic-named royal visitors must be the Maharajah of Cooch Behar, the Gaekwar of Baroda, Prince Antonie D'Orleans, the Infanta d'Espagne, Princess Alexis Dolgourouki and Prince Abrahim. All of these walked up through the Metropole's front entrance in its early days. In the 1840s, revolutions across the Continent led to Brighton becoming a home for foreign exiled royalty and leaders such as Prince Metternich, Princess Lieven and Louis-Philippe.

Sporting Successes

From its earliest days as a resort Brighton and Hove has had to provide sporting activities for visitors, and here we shall celebrate the city's love of sports – those famous and those less so. We start with the ancient game of cricket. Sussex's wonderful County Cricket Ground has been at its present site in Eaton Road

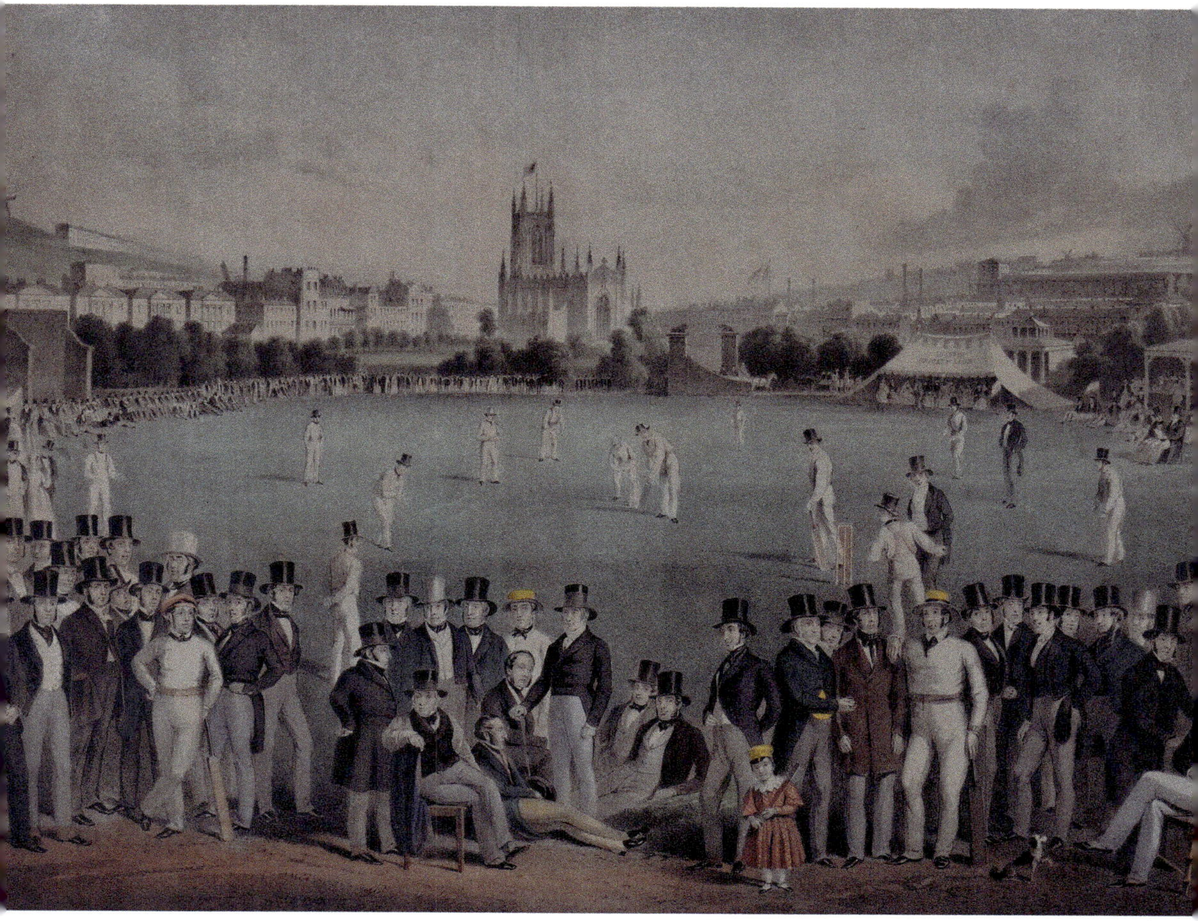

A cricket match at what is now the Level and Park Crescent.

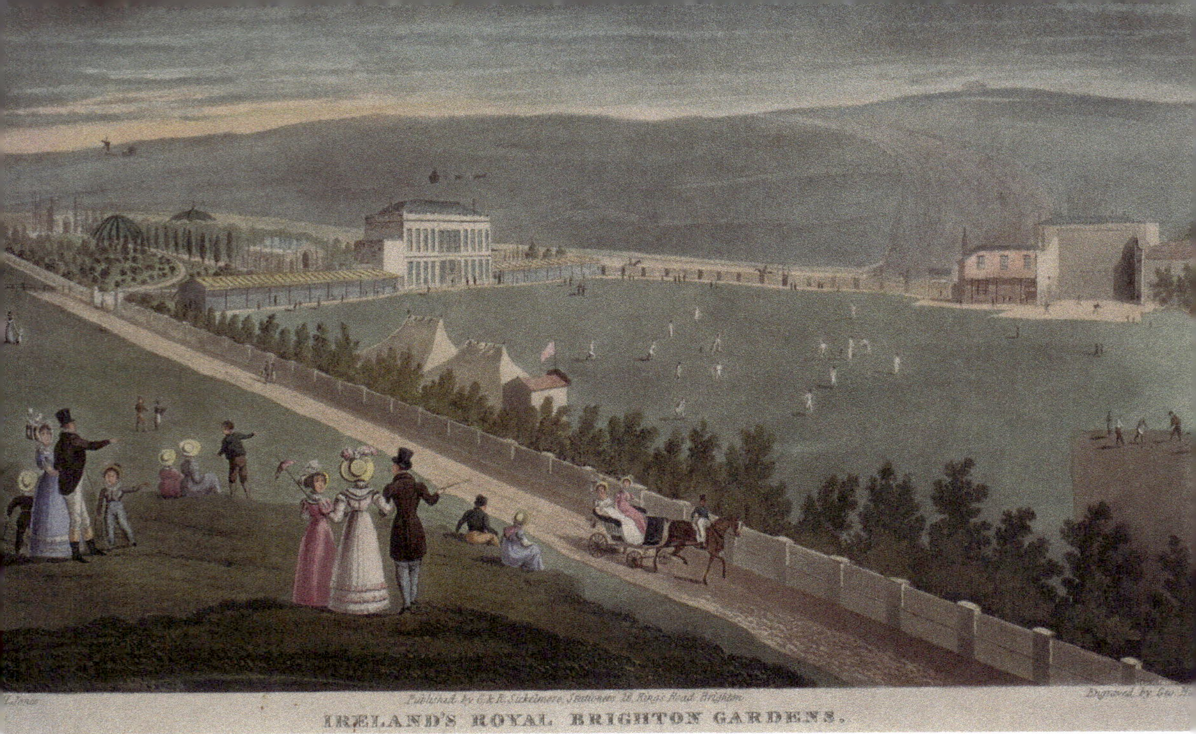

Cricket at the ground by Ireland's Royal Brighton Gardens.

since 1872, before which it was a barley field. Before then it was played on the Downs, Brighton-based at Park Crescent and the Level, and also briefly at the Royal Brunswick Cricket Ground. In this time the ground has overcome many adversities, starting with an invasion by sheep. The first county match was enclosed by a concrete boundary, surrounded by young trees planted nearby. The sheep from a nearby field took a fancy to these and they were never replanted. The ground then survived financial difficulties in its early days when it was in use by a forerunner of the Albion and by two schools, the Belmont and the Claremont, in the 1920s and 1930s. Its hallowed pitch further survived being used for drill when it became the headquarters for the Cyclist Battalion of the Royal Sussex Regiment in the First World War, along with the ice rink that then existed next door. One corner was even used as a rifle range. In the Second World War, it was bombed twice; the first time was in September 1940 and caused four bomb craters and three soldiers to sadly lose their lives during the attempt to diffuse a fifth unexploded bomb. In 1942, during the second raid, the players dived for cover as a small bomb fell by the score box. The ground has even survived sheep dog trials in October 1933, prompting the wonderful old joke that thankfully none of the dogs were found to be guilty.

Before its current location, the County Cricket Ground was based at Temple Fields (where Montpelier Crescent now lies). It was also known as Lee's Trap Ground and then Lilywhite's Ground and opened in 1834, then closed a decade later. Royal Brunswick Ground (where Third and Fourth Avenues are situated) was the third, and finally in 1871 the ground in Eaton Road was acquired from the trustees of the Stanford estate. Turf from the Royal Brunswick Grounds was transferred and relaid on the square, which had been a barley field. Early matches in the 1700s were a comical affair, with teams such as smokers versus non-smokers, batchelors versus married men and family teams. The first County match was played at Eaton Road on 6 June 1872 against Gloucestershire. Even as late as the 1920s a match took place between 'Grocers versus Cobblers'. Sussex CCC has had a successful twenty-first century. The 'Golden Decade', as it is known, is regarded as the club's most successful period since the 1890s, with Sussex reclaiming the County Championship in both 2006 and 2007, as well as making 2006 a 'double' winning year, with the County also winning the C&G trophy in a thrilling low-scoring final at Lord's against Lancashire. The ground also wins you over in being the only one to offer its spectators deckchairs (as you'd expect from a seaside city location), and is the only ground in the country to be floodlit. As Ralph Lewis said, 'Sussex is the cradle of cricket', and this ground has not only a powerful past but a bright future.

Our sporting stars have gone on to great things too. Ex-Brighton and Hove Albion soccer star from the 1980s, Gerry Ryan, wore the club's blue and white shirt when playing for the club and at the club's first FA cup final in 1983, but a career-ending leg injury against Crystal Palace in 1985 meant he swapped that for a landlord's blazer. Ryan took over the Witch Inn in Lindfield in 1987 with his wife Simeon and pride of place above the bar was his Seagulls shirt from the FA cup final. He still turned out regularly for the Witch to play in its team in the Lewes Sunday League. Sadly, Ryan was admitted to hospital on 18 August 2007 following a stroke. Ryan's recovery from the stroke left him with a weakness in his left side and he subsequently sold the Witch.

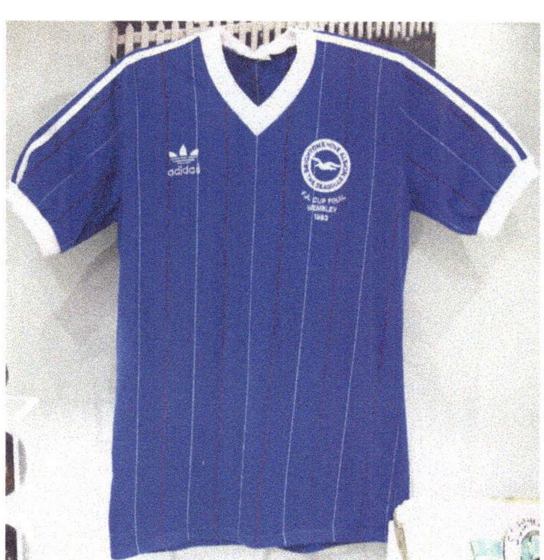
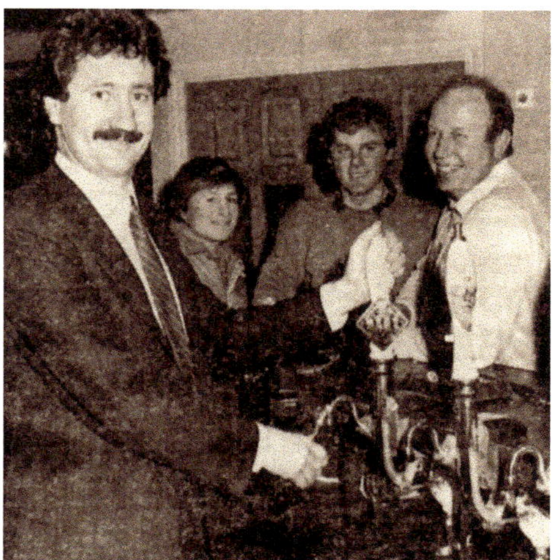

Above left: An Albion shirt from another era when the Seagulls soared high.

Above right: Gerry Ryan. (*The Argus*)

A Selection of Societies and Collection of Clubs

Brighton has boasted a huge number of societies over the centuries. Brighton's aristocratic groups at the time of the Prince Regent included the Choice Spirits, the Humdrums, the Kiddies, Druids, Knights of the Moon, the Pewter Platteronians, the Beef-eating Britons and, my personal favourite, Friends Round the Cauliflower. The most flamboyant of these though was the Bothering Club, presided over by George IV's friend Lord Barrymore. The aim was to annoy in a planned way a guest who was a stranger to Brighton or the Royal Pavilion. Pranks included one Pavilion guest finding a donkey in his room, trussed up by its forelegs to the bedstead with a set of bull's horns attached to its head and several lighted crackers attached to its body. George and the Barrymores draped themselves in tablecloths one night and headdresses of table linen to scare women around the Steine by making mournful noises. Using white table linen again – a shroud or white bedclothes – Barrymore's favourite joke was to wrap up something resembling a body in a coffin, placing it in a lidless coffin and leaning it slightly against someone's front door so when opened a dead body appeared to fall into the house. Barrymore would even dress himself up in his kitchen maid's clothes to attend events.

The first ever Brighton conference was actually at the Royal Pavilion, just after the town had purchased it in 1853. The Pavilion and Town Hall jointly hosted the 1853 meeting of the British Association for the Advancement of Science. As a political party with roots back to the 1600s, you would have thought that the Liberals would have come to such a liberal city for their conference earliest, but in fact the first party to hold their conference here were the Conservatives in 1875. The Liberals were even beaten by the Labour Party by forty-two years, first meeting here in 1921. The Liberals, who returned to Brighton in their current form as the Liberal Democrats in 2020 for their annual conference, only first visited in 1963. Brighton bounced back from the 1984 IRA bombing of the Grand. The Tories continued to book Brighton for their conferences and an estimated 350,000 delegates and visitors came to the town who were linked to the conferences just four years later in 1988. Even then, nearly thirty years ago,

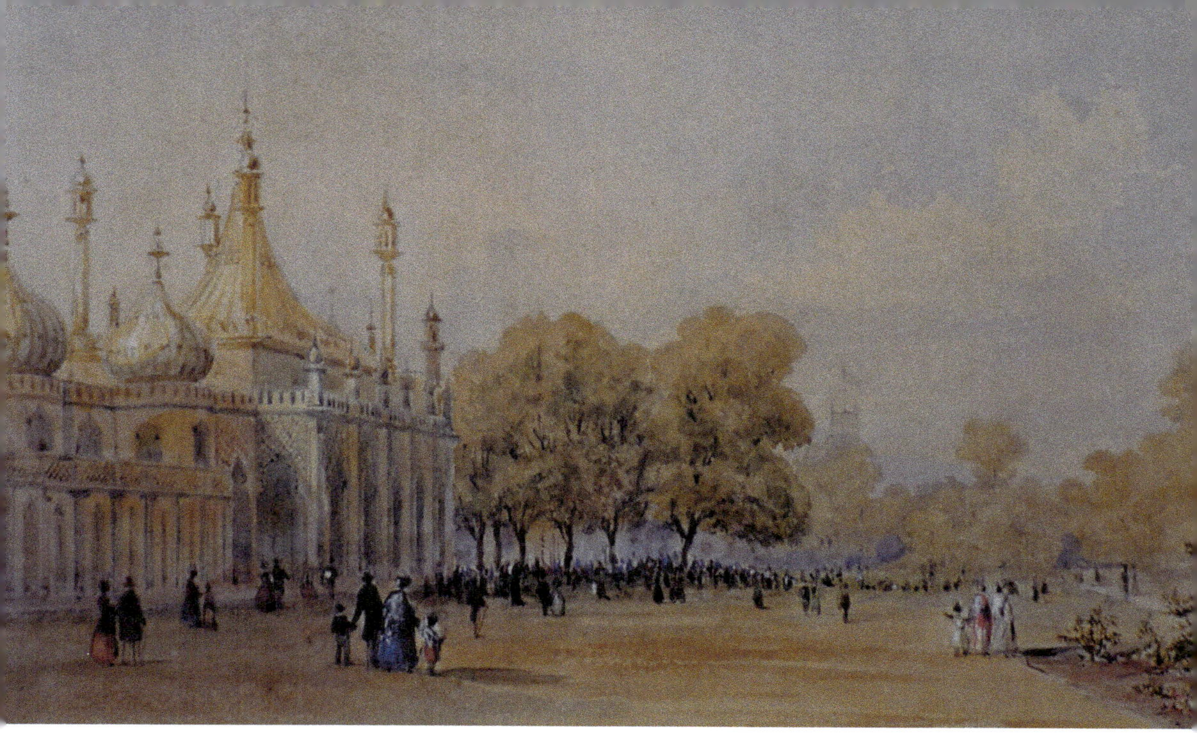

Above: The Royal Pavilion grounds.

Below: Brighton's classical Town Hall.

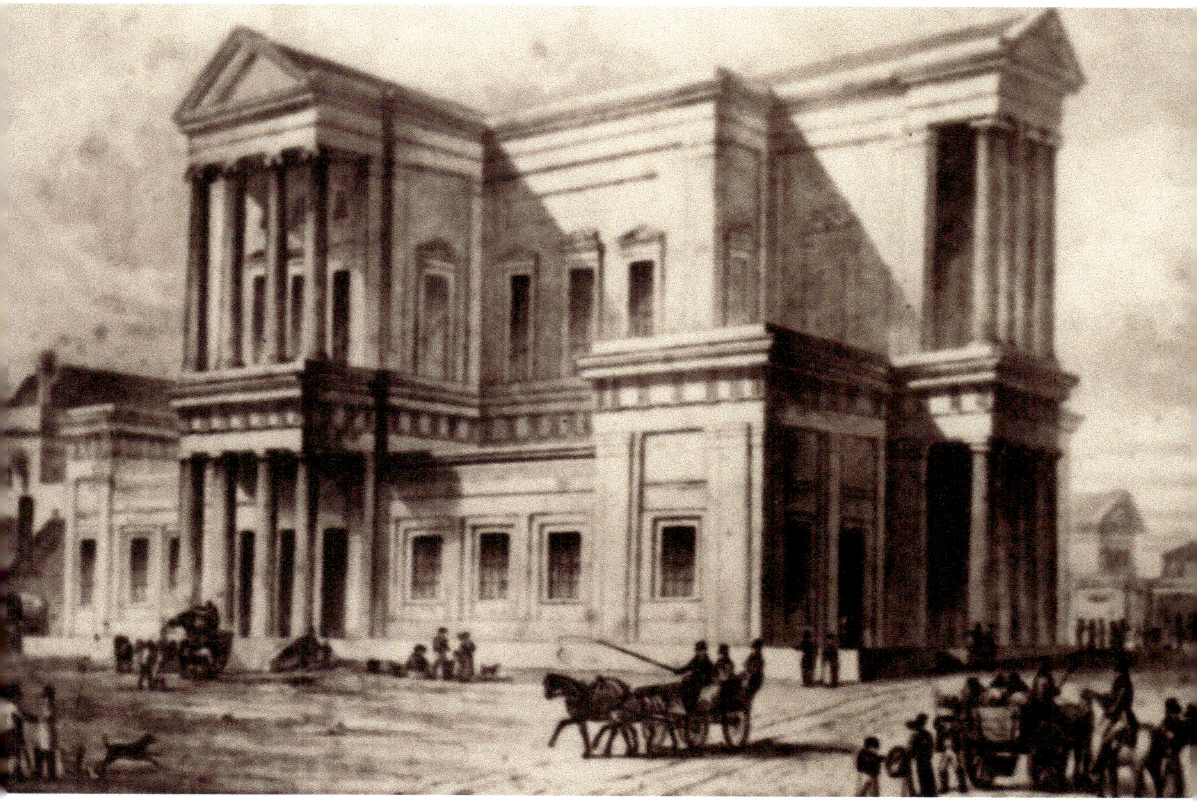

the conference trade was worth at least £53 million to the town. Today, with the Labour conference alone returning alternate years and taking up the Metropole, Grand and Brighton Centre, as well as populating many other hotels and venues, Brighton benefits greatly from our conference trade.

Since 1983 whenever visiting Brighton for its party conference the Labour Party has used the Metropole as its main headquarters when in town. Perhaps the Metropole's red brick and terracotta matches the party's colour better? The first year the party made the move; however, it meant that Labour had to share the hotel with the Psychics and Mystics Fair, which 'promised to tell you all you wanted to know about the future'. Obviously, they weren't able to predict for Labour that they would lose the next two elections, or if they did the new leader elected that year – Neil Kinnock – refused to listen. Labour conferences have also taken place when the party wasn't in opposition. In the 1960s Britain's government actually ran from the banqueting room of the Grand Hotel, as Harold Wilson called a full cabinet meeting while the Labour Party conference was in full swing.

A much better-behaved group than politicians who had a branch in Brighton were the Ancient Order of Froth-Blowers. This drinking and fundraising group was formed in 1924 in Fittleworth. Membership gave you a booklet and card

Brighton's red-brick and terracotta jewel: the Hotel Metropole.

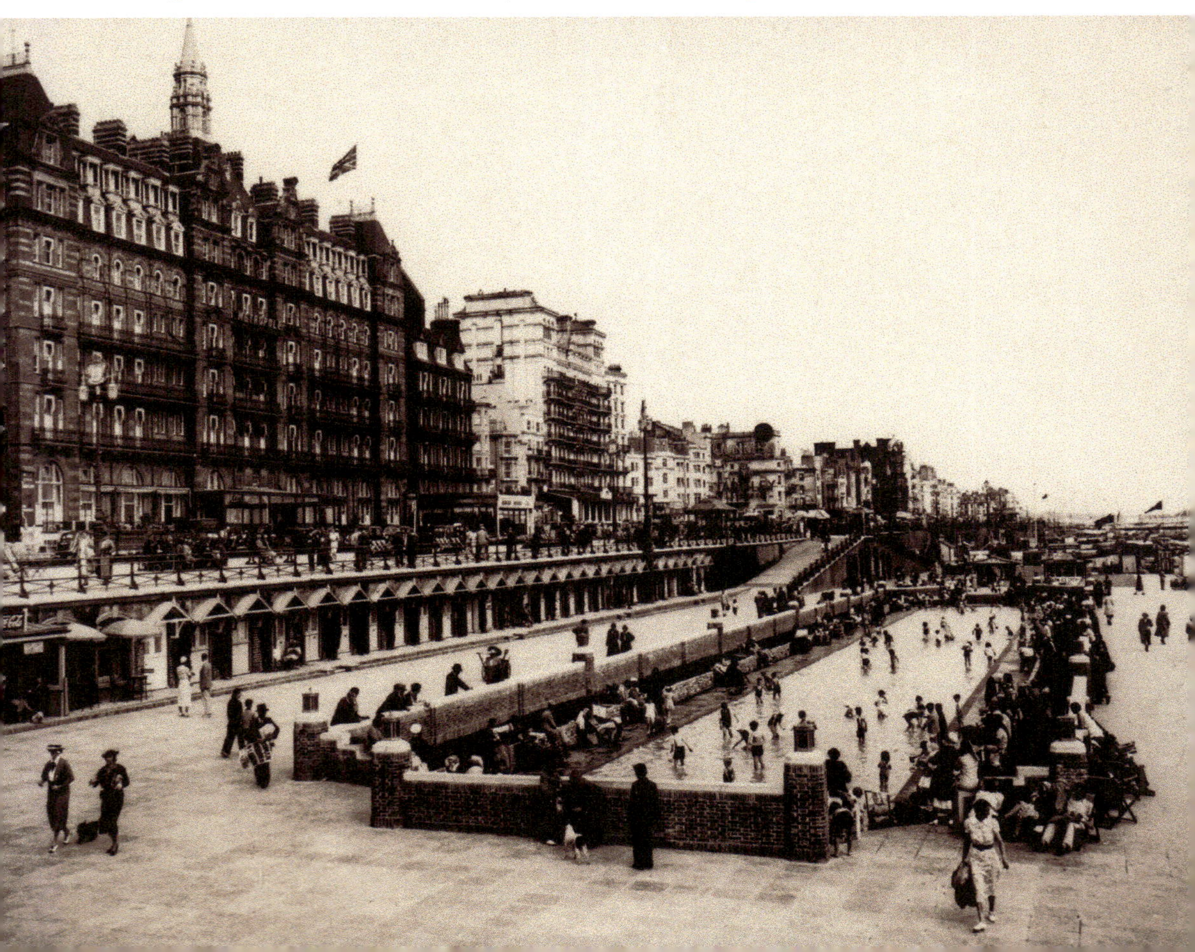

entitling you to 'blow froth off any member's beer' and 'occasionally off non-members' beer provided they are not looking or are of a peaceful disposition'. This trend of daft societies continues today at Sussex University with the Pirate Society. Their webpage informs you of the following:

> So, ye be lookin' to join The Pirate Society, eh? A solid choice if there ever was one. We be most proud of ye for this wise decision. Before ye embark on the journey of a lifetime, be askin' yerself these questions:
>
>> Do ye seek fun and adventure? Do ye dream of a world where ye aren't bound by societal norms and conventions? Do ye want to meet fun loving, thrill seeking, adventure taking individuals like yerself? Do ye want to do all this (and more) dressed as a pirate?
>>
>> If ye be answerin' aye to any of these queries, then The Pirate Society be the place for ye! But even if yer lily-livered self-answered nay to every single one of these 'ere quanderings, the events we be hosting throughout the year are shipshape and sure to turn the heads of all ye land lubbers! Don't be left on a desert island, read on to find the real treasures!

Those hoping to join the group can apparently find 'a welcoming group of individualistic individuals, and a fun, carefree and inclusive environment with something for everyone'. But, most importantly, 'Pirates. Absolutely. Everywhere.'

And who doesn't want to live in a world like that?

Acknowledgements

Images courtesy of the Royal Pavilion and Museums, Brighton and Hove. Other images from archives of *The Argus* and the author's collection.

Many thanks again to Angeline, my editor, for all her fantastic work over the years; Jenny for her huge efforts here with design; and Phillip for his toil with publicity for the book as always. Thanks to fellow local historian Duncan Cameron for his insight into the Isetta factory, and definitely to Kevin Bacon for his help at the Royal Pavilion and Museums, Brighton and Hove again to allow us to have so many mighty fine images. Without the generous help of the archive, this book wouldn't look half as good. To Laura, Seth and Eddie, my love of course.

About the Author

Kevin Newman is a historian, lecturer, teacher and tour guide who when not writing books for Amberley takes individuals and groups on tours of Brighton and Sussex. He has written GCSE history resources and textbooks for schools and his next national book for Amberley is *Clock Towers of England*. His next local history book is *A–Z of Worthing* and should you wish to attend one of his talks or tours, please contact info@allinclusivehistory.org, or call 07504 863867.

Also by the Author
A–Z of Brighton and Hove
Brighton and Hove in 50 Buildings
Lewes Pubs
Secret Brighton
50 Gems of Sussex
Historic England: Sussex
Historic England: Brighton and Hove

Upcoming
A–Z of Worthing
Clock Towers of England